POETRY COMP

GREAT MINDS

Your World...Your Future...YOUR WORDS

From Devon
Edited by Jessica Woodbridge

First published in Great Britain in 2005 by:
Young Writers
Remus House
Coltsfoot Drive
Peterborough
PE2 9JX
Telephone: 01733 890066
Website: www.youngwriters.co.uk

All Rights Reserved

© *Copyright Contributors 2005*

SB ISBN 1 84602 072 7

Foreword

This year, the Young Writers' 'Great Minds' competition proudly presents a showcase of the best poetic talent selected from over 40,000 up-and-coming writers nationwide.

Young Writers was established in 1991 to promote the reading and writing of poetry within schools and to the youth of today. Our books nurture and inspire confidence in the ability of young writers and provide a snapshot of poems written in schools and at home by budding poets of the future.

The thought, effort, imagination and hard work put into each poem impressed us all and the task of selecting poems was a difficult but nevertheless enjoyable experience.

We hope you are as pleased as we are with the final selection and that you and your family continue to be entertained with *Great Minds From Devon* for many years to come.

Contents

Devonport High School For Girls
    Hannah Partridge (12)   1
    Lucy Boyes (15)   2

Exeter School
    Jonathan Frost (11)   2
    Tom Harrill (14)   3
    William Slade (11)   4
    Laurence Trollope (14)   5
    Bryn Walsh (11)   5
    Alice Johnson (12)   6
    Shaun Prankerd (11)   7
    Beatrice Bowles-Bray (11)   7
    Tom Hall (11)   8
    George Greenwood (11)   8
    Lucy James (11)   9
    Jacob Crouch (12)   9
    Edmund Wilkinson (14)   10
    Laurence Hanoman (14)   11
    Ollie Stephenson (11)   11
    Alex Worthington (14)   12
    Will Pring (14)   13
    Callum Stevens (12)   13
    Phyllida Cligg (11)   14
    Amy Glanvill (12)   14
    Alice Brookes (11)   15
    Jethro White (12)   15
    Tim Owens (15)   16
    James Conn (11)   16
    Will Cummings (14)   17
    Samara Lawrence (11)   17
    Aidan Smallwood (14)   18
    Oliver Bedford (11)   18
    David Bird (14)   19
    Simon Hewett (14)   19
    Charlie Palmer (14)   20
    Sam Freeman (14)   21
    Gary Clapson (14)   21
    Edwin Cawthron (14)   22

Great Torrington Community School

Sean Borland (11)	22
Suzanne Nicholson (11)	23
Charles Mill (12)	23
Deborah Tucker (11)	24
Tom Hunt (11)	24
Charlie Banfield (11)	24
Tyler Pollard (11)	25
Bonny Davies (12)	25
Zac Sanders (11)	26
Amy Toop (11)	26
Billie Tubb (12)	26
Fiona Nicholls (13)	27
Alex Gillespie (12)	27
Alex Keeley (12)	27
Leticia Kent (11)	28
Tom Gooch (11)	28
David Andrew (11)	29
Sean Letheren (11)	29
Siân Davies (11)	30
Lindsay McLeod (12)	30
Daniel Copp (11)	31
Ross Gallagher (11)	31
Hannah Jury (11)	32
James Mill (12)	32
Jazmine Ker (11)	33
Bethany Nancekivell (11)	33
Nicole Rous (12)	33
Aidan Barnes (11)	34
Kieran Ford (11)	34
Stuart Allin (11)	34
Samuel Kinsella (11)	35
Stephanie Garner (12)	35
Evie Page (11)	35
Josh Hughes (12)	36
Eleanor Stacey (12)	36
Jessica Blythe (12)	37
Alex Bluck (11)	37
Jack Gilbert (11)	37
Daniel Simpson (11)	38
Miriam Kimber (11)	38
Tasmin Bidgway (11)	39

Josh Day (11)	39
Samantha Bond (12)	39
Owen Ward (12)	40
Emma Edgecombe (11)	40
William Bennett (11)	41
Teresa Beakhouse (11)	41
Lydia Fallaize (12)	42
Sam Nicholls (11)	42
Jade Courtney (12)	43
Ben Harper (11)	43
Seraphina Plows (12)	44
Bryony Porter (11)	44
Samuel Thorp (11)	44
Hannah Parkinson (11)	45
Matthew Waterson (11)	45
Eloise Loufer (11)	45
Rae Cornwall (11)	46
Claire Sanders (11)	47
Jacob Niklasson (11)	47
Krystina Heistercamp (11)	48
Stacey-Ella Freemantle (12)	48
Philippe Pauchet (12)	48
Daniel Stubbs	49
Natalie Day (12)	49
Elliot Brant (12)	49
David Quinn (11)	50
Kathryn Masterson (12)	50
Kimberley Harding (12)	50
Adam Bewes (12)	51
Megan Avery (11)	51
Ruby Heywood (12)	52
Josh Jones (11)	52
Katie Mills (12)	53
Bryony Peachey (12)	54
Jemimah Lane (13)	55
Yasmin Clarke-Collins (13)	55
Kirsty Spear (12)	56
Jessica Matthews (13)	56
Megan Chesters (13)	57
Kelvin Lancaster (12)	57
Toni Alexander (13)	58
Karl Knight (12)	58

Lauren Priest (13)	59
Sian Bartlett (12)	59
Annie Ritson (12)	60
Luke Daniel (12)	60
Amy Crocker (12)	61
Charlotte Jeffery (12)	62
Matthew Webber (12)	62
Joshua Goaman (12)	62
Blyth Bosher (12)	63
James Fishleigh (12)	63
Owen Dell (12)	63
Billy Curtis (12)	64
Lauren Slater (12)	64

Grenville College

Lydia Singer (11)	65
Rebekah Locke (11)	65
Tom Marsden (11)	65
William Shortridge (11)	66
Chloe MacGillivray (11)	66
Daniel Rogerson (11)	67
Georgina Barrington (11)	67
Oliver White (12)	68
Jonathan Brookes (11)	68
Ebony Gunn (12)	69
Sarah Hookway (13)	69
Rachel Wingate (13)	70
James Guilfoyle (12)	70
Lyndon Wake (14)	71
Joanna Lock (13)	71
Holly Rampling (12)	72
Vicki Withecombe (13)	72
Eleanor Briggs (13)	73
Michelle Dymond (13)	74
Nicholas Deakes (13)	75
Mark Murgelas (13)	75
Joshua Minici (12)	76
Harry Swannack (12)	76
Emma Corrick (12)	77
Nicolle Hockin (12)	77
Aaron Penn (13)	78

Abigail Taylor (12)	78
Sam Petty (12)	79
Charlotte Handley (12)	79
Samuel Smith (13)	80
George Snell (12)	80
Fiona Webb (13)	81
Josh Taylor (13)	81

Hele's School

Imogen Strachan (14)	82
Kate Rivers (16)	83
Abigail Ings (14)	83
Laura Rice (12)	84
Amy Townsend (12)	84
Gemma Stewart (13)	85
Kurt Richards (13)	86
Alexa Parker-Carn (11)	87
Hannah Moran (12)	88
Hannah Hart (11)	89
Matthew Bloomfield (11)	89
Rebekah Cunningham (12)	90
Charlotte Bromley (11)	90

Ilfracombe College

Holly Meaden (11)	91
Georgina Hill (11)	92
Vicky Ratcliff (14)	92
Amy Batstone (13)	93
Rickie Adcock (12)	94

King Edward VI Community College

James Neubert (11)	94
Charlotte Fisher (13)	95
Poppy Struben (12)	96
Betsy Porritt (16)	97
Harriet Dodd (12)	98

Lipson Community College

Amy Williams (12)	98
Ryan McCarthy (12)	99

Paul Decourcey (13)	100
Alexander Williams (12)	100
Ben Gomersall (12)	101
Reece Chamberlain (12)	101
Leah Doidge (12)	102
Jodine Bunker (12)	102
Mark Davis (13)	103
Leah Webb (12)	103
Nicola James (12)	104
Jannine Penny (13)	104
Ben Higgins (12)	105
Emma Johnson (13)	105
Sophia Lidstone (13)	106
Joanne Hookins (12)	106
Shadene Lewis (13)	107
Jason Haswell (13)	107
Declan Kehoe (13)	108
Lana Vaughan (12)	109
Dayne Paull (12)	110
Georgina Gue (12)	111
Tia Britton (12)	111
Abigail Gallagher (12)	111
Rebecca Smith (12)	112
Jamie Hall (13)	112
Alexandra May (12)	113
Gavin Price-Horne (12)	113
Scott Robson (12)	114
Sumaya Muganzi (12)	114
Jodi Smith (12)	115
Patrick Sweeting (12)	115

Longcause Community Special School

Chesney Wilkes (13)	116
Sarah Brimacombe (14)	116
Alex Lang (13)	117
Patrick Baldry-Lee (13)	117
Oliver Smith (13)	118
Daniel Huxham (13)	118
Gary Beasley (14)	119
Zoe O'Connor (13)	119

Paignton Community College
Demelza Champion (13) 120
Carl Harding (12) 120
Tristan Illman (13) 121
Sita Zapata (12) 121
Lloyd Porter (12) 122
Craig Hughes (12) 122
Jo Parnell (13) 123
Lisa Williams (12) 124
Kelly Knight (12) 125
Melanie Jenkins (13) 125
Elliot Simpson (12) 126
Mitch Duffin (12) 126
Emma Gallacher (13) 127
Lauren White (12) 127
Thomas Parker (12) 128
Nathan German (13) 128
Natasha Perry (12) 129
Holly Hill (12) 129
Vicki Wilding (12) 130
Katie Callam (12) 130
Leanne Hardwell (11) 131
Isla Fawcett (12) 131
Sophie Greedus (12) 132
Katie O'Brien (12) 132
Marcus Ogborne (12) 133
Jack Williams (12) 133
Dominique Carr (13) 134
James Washbrook (12) 134
Sam Dennis (13) 135
Alexandra Keen (12) 135
Lauren Simpson (14) 136
Katy Biggins (13) 136
Jade Cooper (14) 137
Joanne Butler (13) 137
Emily Brown (13) 138
Samantha Gardner (14) 138
Hannah Wilson (13) 139
Ilan Adam Strul (11) 140
Michael Bradfield-Payne (13) 141
Jade Hodgkinson (13) 141

Sady Boswell (14)	142
Emma Louise Bilski (13)	143
Amber Baird (11)	143
Fiona Bell (12)	144
Joanne Mills (12)	144
Vaneese Cox (12)	145
Chris Lawes (12)	145
Connor Mills (12)	146
Emily Powell (12)	146
Matthew Jerwood (12)	147
Paul Buckley (12)	148
Lydia Hardy (12)	149
Benjamin Gerrish (12)	149
Danielle Goldthorpe	150
Jordan Victoria Jones (12)	150
Laura Searson (13)	151
Stacey Brown (11)	151
Jade Oaff (12)	152
Lauren Cooper (12)	152
Lloyd Franklin (12)	153
Tracey Landry (12)	153
Shaun Ellis (12)	153
Maxine Halcro (13)	154
Katie Moores	154
Emily Penwarden (12)	155
Jemma Brown (12)	155
Charles Stanley-Bloom (12)	156
Rose-Marie Timms (12)	156
Ellis Platt-Lea (12)	157
Chris Baker (13)	157
Claire Smith (13)	158
Stuart Dearson (13)	158
Luke Steward (12)	159
Rachel Mussett (12)	159
Robert Michael Roskelley (12)	160
Charlotte Brown (13)	160
Ethan Wilkins (11)	160
Darell Andrews (13)	161
Lindsey Evans (13)	161
Ami Hopkins (13)	162
Sophie Poole (11)	162
Simon Nicholls (11)	162

Jordan Colledge (13)	163
Dale Steadman (12)	163
Michael Hughes (11)	163
Hannah Cooney (12)	164
David Healy (11)	164
Bryony Young (11)	164
Hannah Gladman (13)	165
Harry Clay (14)	165
Emily Barnett (13)	166
Catherine Hougardy (13)	166
Adam Westwood (13)	167
Katie Rees (12)	167
Ashley Millar (12)	168
Stephen Swann (12)	168

St James' High School, Exeter

Sadie Robinson (13)	168
Cogan Westlake	169
Zara Broughton (12)	170
Aydan Gasimova (12)	171
Jamie Bassett (13)	172
Gemma Toy (12)	172
Ryan Beckett (13)	173
Chloe Meredith (12)	173
Jade Ashelford (12)	174
Lauren Meredith (12)	174

St Luke's High School, Exeter

Jennie Hamer (12)	175
Spike van der Vliet-Firth (12)	175

St Wilfrid's School, Exeter

Katie Snow (11)	176
Philip Birrell (11)	176
Chantal Payne (12)	177
Natasha Durman (11)	177
Jordan Wills (11)	178
Luke Oliver (11)	179
Ashton Snow (11)	180

South Dartmoor Community College
Erik Jellyman (13)	180
Jaye Noble-John (13)	181
Fern Rhys (18)	182
Leonora Wood (13)	183

Teignmouth Community College
Sophia Rose Oliver (13)	184
Laura Holland (13)	185
Sarah Olding (13)	186

Torquay Boys' Grammar School
Scott Parnell (13)	187
Tom Porch (12)	188
Roger Doxat-Pratt (12)	189
Sam Grace (12)	190
Alex Hambis (12)	191
Josh Papanicola (13)	192
William Kember (13)	193
Matthew Mowat (12)	194
Jay Spencer (17)	195
Zac Clark (12)	196
Paul Moroz (11)	197
Shaun Minto (13)	198
Simon Ward (17)	199
Mark Buffey (13)	200
David Benson (13)	201
Charlie Hornsby (12)	202
Matthew West (12)	203
Richard Petty (12)	204
James Bourne (13)	205
Thomas Uddin (13)	206

Torquay Grammar School For Girls
Polly Brown (12)	207
Charlotte Slough (12)	208
Jessica Levinson Young (12)	209
Ellen Harber (12)	210
Chloe Avery (12)	210
Libby Feist (12)	211

Ellie May (11)	211
Deborah Mason (12)	212
Lauren Perriton (11)	212
Hannah Reeves (12)	213
Elizabeth Hunt (12)	213
Charlotte Dyer (12)	214
Sarah Whittaker (12)	214
Amy Harding (12)	215
Olivia Mae Jaremi (11)	215
Ellie Wilde (11)	216
Sophia Peutherer (11)	217
Abigail Fryett (12)	217
Amy Goldman (12)	218
Serena Gosden (11)	218
Debbie White (12)	219
Gabriella Strange (16)	220
Amy Edwards (11)	220
Sarah Snow (12)	221
Melissa King (11)	221
Hannah Williams (11)	222
Lily Partridge (11)	222
Vicky Wilton (11)	223
Jessica Woodhead (11)	223
Kathryn McGhee (11)	224
Kelly Butler (12)	225
Charlotte Davey (11)	225
Cicely Wills (11)	226
Christina Webber (11)	227
Anna Burlace (11)	227
Roxanne Hughes (11)	228
Sam Urban (11)	228
Kristina Homer (11)	229
Annabel Seymour (12)	229
Hannah Dennison (16)	230
Georgina McLennan (11)	230
Rebecca Stanley (13)	231
Hollie Dennison (11)	231
Haidee Badcott (13)	232
Rebekah Keating (12)	233
Bethany Clarke (11)	233
Rosie Gibbes (12)	234
Victoria Harris (12)	234

Sophie Thompson (12)	235
Nathalie Baker (12)	236
Jade Elms (12)	236
Helen Bovey (12)	237
Rebecca Polding (12)	237
Gabriela Lancaster (12)	238
Hannah Short (12)	238
Sarah New (12)	239
Chantelle Lee (11)	239
Juliet Wheeler (11)	240
Katie Girow (11)	241
Georgina Picot (12)	242
Victoria Harvey (11)	242
Hannah Zebrowski (12)	243
Charlie Bendall (11)	243
Lottie Smith (12)	244
Harriet Blackborow (11)	244
Natalie Dingle (13)	245
Jessica Clarke (12)	245
Victoria Hammond (12)	246
Jessica Calf (12)	246
Vikki Chammings (11)	247
Shannon Gribble (11)	247
Joanna Beck (11)	247
Katie Smith (12)	248
Faye Dadson (11)	248
Jessica Simpson (12)	249
Rebecca Squires (11)	249
Matilda Naylor (12)	250
Michelle Nixon (11)	250
Chloe Holloway (11)	251
Ellie Hone (11)	251
Vicky Smart (12)	252
Lillie Barnett (11)	252

Trinity School

Hannah Wilce (12)	253
Emma Bascombe (12)	253
Alexandra Turner (12)	254
Rachel Gates (11)	255
Katrina Godden (13)	255

Abby Coombes (12)	256
Kim Rogers (13)	256
Rebecca Robbins (12)	257
Matthew Childs (13)	257
Sarah Smith (13)	258
Jasmin Salmon (12)	258
Ashley Ladd (13)	259
Charlie Penny (13)	259
Jess Whitworth (14)	260
James Hatch (13)	260
Graham Gilmour (14)	261
William Doble (13)	261
Gemma Edgecombe (13)	262
Emma Long (13)	262

Woodlands School

Lewys Tapscott Nott (13)	262
Ashley Card (13)	263
Keith Persey (13)	263
Ben Morfey (11)	264
Claire Jury (12)	264
Reece Dorrall (12)	265
Jemma Watts (11)	265
Josh Morfey (11)	266
Kieran Double (11)	266

The Poems

Great Minds

Some can do division,
Or creatively write,
Some can lift weights,
Or just try with all their might!

Some can ride horses,
Or run very fast,
Some can climb trees
And end up with a cast!

Some can teach swimming,
Or remember a day,
Some can do boxing
And still be okay!

Some can draw pictures,
Or convincingly lie,
Some can do the splits,
I don't know why!

Some can make cookies,
Or can build a boat,
Some can eat Brussels sprouts,
I certainly don't!

Some can educate children,
Or can just amuse them,
We all have great minds,
It's just how you use them!

Hannah Partridge (12)
Devonport High School for Girls

Thoughts Of A Dying Inventor

Oh, but the air is filled with the bitter tang of loneliness,
All lost, all gone, and none remain,
By my side are empty spaces, faces haunt my mind,
But no more can I lay claim to this fading glory,
No longer is this passionless conviction mine,
They took it, and they tore it to shreds,
Now like grey confetti, dampened in fog and wind,
Does my success flit and flutter about my face,
These bird-like ghosts are my past, my present
But never can they be my future,
I have no future, nor any want of one,
My story ends here tonight,
And I leave you all my possessions, and just one wish,
When in years to come my name is carved into encyclopaedic tomes,
I ask that you write this:
'He was a great man, a great mind, a great figure,
And an icon of all that could never be'.

Lucy Boyes (15)
Devonport High School for Girls

Nonsense Poem

I saw a skeleton running across the grass,
I saw a rabbit eating chips,
I saw an American rolling down a hill,
I saw a ball cast off,
I saw a ship fly by,
I saw an aeroplane eat a sausage,
I saw a dog with a chainsaw,
I saw a madman with green leaves,
I saw a tree walking the dog,
I saw a man eating acorns,
I saw a squirrel playing Frisbee,
I saw a boy munching leaves,
I saw the caterpillar who saw these things
And I wonder what he made of it.

Jonathan Frost (11)
Exeter School

Who's Who?

Thomas Harrill you are omnipotent,
You are wonderful, overpowering, and imposing,
You are the god of gods,
You are the creator of creators,
You are the king of the jungle,
You are the alligator and the lion,
The unicorn and the eagle,
You are the colours of the spectrum,
You are black, and you are white,
You are the day, and you are the night,
You are the creator and the conductor,
You are the dictator of the universe,
Behold the eyes of Thomas Harrill,
Shiny coals that harbour wisdom like no other,
Behold his divine skeletal structure,
Built stronger than diamonds, unbreakable and impenetrable,
Angels bow on bended knee at the sound of your name,
In this world Thomas Harrill
Noster pater,
Fidei defensor,
Dei gratia,
You are so much more than these weak compliments,
Beside your figure the sun is embarrassed to shine,
For your highness is so intense, every star in the universal
Structure of infinity seems dimmed.
Thomas Harrill, the planets echo your name,
The electrons, protons and neutrons, written in your name,
You, Thomas Harrill, are the universe
And the universe is you.

Tom Harrill (14)
Exeter School

The Fight With The Minotaur

The Minotaur stood in the cave,
The loin cloth round his waist,
His bloodshot eyes and steaming ears,
Made him look quite fierce.

Around me lay the corpses
And the bodies there'd once been.
The urine and the stale sweat
Were the audience of the scene.

The death was travelling through the air
And flying through my brain.
I knew what I must do to win
Though I could feel the pain.

The blood, the fear, the bones and sweat,
The victory was not near.
I aimed a blow at the Minotaur's chest
But missed and cut his ear.

The Minotaur charged with sharp, white horns,
Rock fell all around,
I hit the horns with my sword
Which clattered to the ground.

I edged back over bones,
The crunch rang through my ears.
I grabbed the sword and felt the hilt
In my hand again.

I plunged the sword into his chest,
The screams rang through the cave.
The Minotaur fell to his knees
And blood dripped off my sword.

William Slade (11)
Exeter School

Legends Shall Be Re-Written

Laurence Trollope you are superior,
It was you who pulled Ra's chariot across the sky,
It is you who brings light to life,
The light you create guides the world towards you,
You are the Alpha and Omega,
You are the beginning and the end,
You are the first and the last,
You are the creator of time and the end of the universe,
Isis smiles her blessings upon you,
Set bestows his powers to you,
Ptah kneels to the true creator of everything, you,
You are neither Zeus nor his son but the creator of matter,
The seas aren't merely under Poseidon's control, but yours,
Hades fears you for he knows of true power,
His soul is corrupted but yours shall dance with the angels,
The mighty Thor bows down at his true emperor
And lays down his hammer in honour of your grand might,
You are Yggdrasil, the great ash tree of life,
Those who oppose you, go straight into the open jaws of Fenrir.
And those who love you are many,
And you bless them for you are all powerful and all seeing,
These gods walk as children, while you walk as man.
You are birth and death,
You are the sunrise and the sunset.

Laurence Trollope (14)
Exeter School

I Love My Dog With An H

I love with my dog with an H
Because she is hilarious,
Hairy
And harmless.
Her name is Henrietta,
She lives in Hereford
And eats hermit crabs happily.

Bryn Walsh (11)
Exeter School

Fight For Life

The dark, damp cave surrounds me,
A shudder of fear runs down my spine.
The smell of rotting corpses invade my nostrils,
The beast lies sleeping,
Fur matted with victim's blood.
Sword in hand I creep forward,
My arm raised to strike,
My heart races,
Blood pounds in my brain,
Huge bloodshot eyes spring open,
I taste fear!

A deafening *roar!* echoes in the cave,
I cry out in terror,
The scrabble of claws on stone,
The beast looms over me.
The crunching of bones
Under the Minotaur's paws.
Sounds like chalk on a blackboard,
His horns pierce my flesh
As he charges into me,
Agony breaks from my lips,
Falling weak and feeble against the wet, mossy wall.

The beast thunders towards me,
I muster strength to strike,
The mighty blade flashes in the half-light,
I strike the beast,
His head flies from his shoulders,
A cry of victory breaks from my bloodied mouth,
I have defeated the Minotaur.

Alice Johnson (12)
Exeter School

The Senses Of Battle

The things I touched,
The blade of my sword covered in blood,
The motionless leg of the monster
And the skull of the beast,
All these things I touched,
Made me feel victory.

The things I smelt,
The smell of blood,
Death, rotting teeth and the body,
Rotting already, all these smells
Led to the smell of victory.

The things I taste
Of the monster's blood,
His fur in my mouth,
The taste of my own spit,
All these lead
To the taste of victory.

The sounds I hear,
The sounds of those killed now cheering,
Falling rocks,
Splashing and crunching as I walk to the entrance,
All these sounds are sounds of victory.

Shaun Prankerd (11)
Exeter School

I Love My Puppy With An S

I love my puppy with an S
Because he's a sensation, serene
And sweet!
His name is Saul,
He lives in the sea
And gobbles all the scallops for tea.

Beatrice Bowles-Bray (11)
Exeter School

Fatal Fight

Smell of blood and sweat,
Faeces randomly scattered,
Fleshy, greasy hands the sizes of plates,
Red, bloodshot eyes,
Sharpened horns,
Swish of sword,
Stinking, snorting breath,
Screams of half-dead victims,
Manky fur, sticky air,
Incessant flies,
Thrust of my sword,
Roar of pain,
Arms jarred,
Dig further until I hit bone,
Wrench my weapon free,
It lies dead in its stone graveyard.

Tom Hall (11)
Exeter School

Smokey

I love my grandmother's cat with an S
Because he slashes
At string,
Sneaking and scaling,
Skidding and leaping.
Staying still,
Ready to pounce,
His name is Smokey
And he moves like smoke
Sliding about
Sinuously.

George Greenwood (11)
Exeter School

In The Den

Cold, darkened stare,
Bloodshot eyes spoke to me,
Rotting corpses spoke like angels,
Trying to convince the darkness of my mind,
Ragged breathing made me shudder,
Creeping away never to be seen.

Suffocating at the smell,
I gasp aloud,
Nearer,
Nearer,
Here it comes.

Strike!
Slash of sword,
Sound like no other,
The beast,
He dies
On a stalagmite deathbed.

Lucy James (11)
Exeter School

I Love My Dog With An M

I love my dog with an M
Because he is a monstrosity, a monster and a menace.
His name is Mozart,
He lives in Mum's house,
He eats mozzarella, Magnums and mustard,
Mustard makes him *mad!*

Jacob Crouch (12)
Exeter School

I Am The Champion

All beings hail your name Ed Wilkinson,
You are more worthy than God, none are second to you.
You bring the dreams people dream, you are all they ever think of,
Your beauty precedes you for miles on end.
You are a vision of life, as pretty as light on morning dew,
You are perfection in its purest form.
Your eyes are the wells from which wisdom flows
And they bring the fires from Hell.
Your arms are the rocks from which men mine,
Your hair is the forest in which men dwell.
Mountains will stoop for you,
Cities will fall at your feet.
Kings will bow down before you,
Mighty Zeus is second to you,
None can hold a candle to you.
You make the sun rise and set,
You are the wild horses upon the plains, free, golden, unstoppable.
Angels will come to beg for your mercy,
You are the Alpha and Omega.
Legions of men bow down at your feet,
Even Jesus came to try and touch you.
You are the biggest star in the sky,
When the wind whistles, it whistles your name.
You are Heaven's VIP,
Not carpe diem, you are the day,
You are the all, Ed Wilkinson.

Edmund Wilkinson (14)
Exeter School

Who Is Who?

Laurence Hanoman you are simply magnificent,
You are the god of all gods and you put the others to shame.
You are the spirit of the earth, the wind, the fire and the water,
You see no evil,
You hear no evil,
You speak no evil,
You are the Alpha and the Omega,
The moon and stars fall at your feet,
You are invisible,
You are unbeatable,
The universe was created for the sole purpose of worshipping you,
No one dares oppose you, for you would grind them into the dust
Like a dying creature, doomed to die.
Your stare burns through the eyes of mortals,
Casting a burning glow over the world.
Your hands crush the demons of Hell
And Heaven created the halo above your head.
You are the one and only,
You are the one,
You are Laurence Hanoman.

Laurence Hanoman (14)
Exeter School

I Love My Brother With An E

I love my brother with an E
Because he is ecstatic,
Never an Eskimo,
His name is Elfer,
He lives in England
And is always equilateral about erasing.

Ollie Stephenson (11)
Exeter School

No One Is Worthy

Alex Worthington you are the Omega,
You are the bringer of happiness,
Bringer of joy,
Bringer of fear,
Bringer of beer,
Bringer of nectar drink of the gods,
You are too good for it, as you are too good for everyone else,
You are the bridge over troubled water,
You are the Poseidon of the sea,
You are the Zeus of the skies,
You are wiser than Athena, goddess of wisdom,
You are the ruler of the universe,
You are the light in the darkest corners,
You are Alex Worthington.
Your eyes are the stars reflecting bright,
Your hair is as soft as silk,
You are perfection personified,
You are impervious of anger,
You are vaccinated against fear,
You are the riches of kings,
You are the king of riches,
Your name shall be whispered throughout the ages,
Worthy, no one is worthy of you.

Alex Worthington (14)
Exeter School

Will Pring

Will Pring you are a legend,
You are the greatest,
You are the man,
You are the light that lights the world,
You are the world,
You are the man on the face of the moon,
You are the man above Jesus,
You are the man above God,
Without you the world is nothing,
Without you life is nothing,
Without you happiness is obsolete,
Your face is the face on everyone's mind,
Your body the body that everyone craves,
You are the man who everyone loves,
You are the sun,
You are the rain,
You are the plants,
You are the tree in the garden of Eden,
Your place in Heaven is secure,
You Will Pring, are perfection.

Will Pring (14)
Exeter School

I Love My Dog With A D

I love my dog with a D
Because he is determined,
Dangerous and dreaming.
His name is Duggy,
He lives in a disused dishwasher,
He eats doughnut dumplings,
Devilishly.

Callum Stevens (12)
Exeter School

Theseus And The Minotaur

A huge furry body
Arose above me
Like a wave
About to crash.
Roaring like a wildebeest
His giant arms and legs
Flapping around in the air.
The smell of vomit
Surrounded the air.

Rotting bodies merged
With the smell as well,
I could hear the cry of victims,
Ripped and torn apart
With his immense hands.

Blood dripping
From the top of caves,
Muck streaming
In puddles of urine.
Suddenly the Minotaur thudding towards me,
The first strike cuts across his chest.
Blood streams horrendously on the second.
On the third the Minotaur collapses,
Sinks to the ground
Like a falling leaf.

Phyllida Cligg (11)
Exeter School

I Love My Cats With A B

I love my cats with a B
Because they are bonny, beautiful and bouncy.
Their names are Blobby and Bam,
They live in Botswana and go on holiday to Belgium.
They chew on bamboo and drink beer,
But unfortunately they always come home drunk.

Amy Glanvill (12)
Exeter School

The Fight

In the moment I knew my deathbed lay here,
I heard my father's sweet voice,
Came back to my senses,
The sword clattered on the stones.
I heard dripping blood
Pattering gently on the rough rocks.
There, upon the floor,
Lay rotten bodies,
Skeletons and skulls.
The creature's foul breath filled the room
And his waste lay in smoking piles on the floor.
I could smell death!

In my mouth I could taste
A mixture of blood, fur and spittle,
Though my mouth was bitter and dry.
My sweaty, bleeding hands felt the rough fur of the monster.
Its sharp horns pierced through my naked skin,
Spilling fresh blood.
I felt the smooth leather of my sword,
Slipping through my bloodshed hands.
He threw me across his den,
Onto rough stones.

Alice Brookes (11)
Exeter School

I Love My Dog With A D

I love my dog with a D
Because she is determined,
Desirable and devoted,
Her name is Dillon,
She lives in Dundee,
And guzzles down all the deer.

Jethro White (12)
Exeter School

Who's Who?

Owens you are a saint,
You are beautiful, you're the one with the girls,
You are small, but very cool,
You are strong, with a powerful mind.
Owens you are a saint,
Behold the eyes of a saint,
Behold the stars, your community that surrounds you.
Behold you stepping forth.
You have a body like Hercules,
Tu es très anwfant.
You are two steps up from God,
You are two above infinity.
Behold the excellence of your world,
You are like a slave working for excellence.
You are wild horses on a desert's plain,
Unstoppable and on a mission.
You are a fish that will never be extinct,
Owens you are a saint,
We all bow down to you.

Tim Owens (15)
Exeter School

I Saw Nonsense

I saw the love in guilty lies,
I saw the fear in a couple's eyes,
I saw the ghosts in a victim's face,
I saw the courage in a haunted place,
I saw the tears in the winning side,
I saw happiness in someone who cried,
I alone have witnessed these events,
Some were happy and some were tense.

James Conn (11)
Exeter School

The Creator

Will Cummings you are the creator of everything,
You are all things bright and beautiful,
All gods kneel before you,
You are the dweller of the heavens,
You are the bringer of hope and wisdom,
For the creator of everything is Will Cummings,
For whose are the arms of stone?
For whose are the legs which will never kneel?
For whose is the mighty tower within the heavens?
It is Will's.
For the Earth is your country,
For its people are your worshippers,
All legions of armies in every country salute you,
Through your amazing willpower, you are the supreme ruler,
Men and women alike, hold you in the high,
Men even chant the words for you:
Dulce et decorum est pro patria mori,
These words you will need to pass into your glory,
Out of the darkness and into the fire,
Out of the black and into the light,
Into the kingdom of the Lord,
The one and only Will Cummings.

Will Cummings (14)
Exeter School

I Love My Dog With An M

I love my dog with an M
Because she is a marvellous mastermind
And never meditates.
Her name is Milly,
She lives in Menorca,
She eats Milky Ways, melons and meat.

Samara Lawrence (11)
Exeter School

Who Is Who?

Aidan Smallwood you are the best,
You are the brightest star in the sky,
You are the god among gods,
You are the corpus sanctum,
You are perfection personified
In harmony with the ocean, the land and the skies.
You are the loaves and the fishes,
You are the soul of the universe,
You are the light among the dark trees,
Shining in the caves and the depths of the stagnant pools,
The brilliant gem adorning the fairest crown.
You are the great mountain,
Your head is among the clouds,
You are the waves, the sea, the ocean,
You are the cloud, the sky.
Every tree bows down to your thunderous breath,
Your slightest whisper is a joy to the feverish brow.
Every house, every village, every town, every city trembles,
Trembles at the mention of your name.
Every planet, every person, animal, plant
Is refreshed by your heavenly voice.

Aidan Smallwood (14)
Exeter School

I Love My Cat With An . . . ABC

I love my cat with an . . . ABC
Because she is authentic, beloved and cunning,
Acrobatic, bold and curious,
Apprehensive, bashful and clever.
Her name is Acorn Bean Conny,
She lives in Ash Bin in Clover,
She eats adders, boils and lots of corn,
Wearing anorak, boots and cap.

Oliver Bedford (11)
Exeter School

Perfection

You are perfect,
You are god,
You are the passion,
You burn brighter than fire,
Brighter than Hell.
You are Lord over all,
No one can compare,
Every atom,
Every planet
Bows to you.
Your resounding beauty flattens all opposition,
You are the mountains,
You are the trees,
You are the light,
You are the one,
The only,
David Bird,
You are perfection in its purest form.

David Bird (14)
Exeter School

Supreme Lord

Simon Hewett you are the supreme lord,
You are the centre of the universe,
The elements fear your name,
The sea shakes with the sound of your voice,
The trees shrivel up with your touch,
You make other beings seem obsolete,
You control the heavens and the stars,
You are brighter than the sun,
You are the centre of all fears,
You are the people's hope,
You are what the people live for,
Without you the world has no meaning.

Simon Hewett (14)
Exeter School

Whispers

Charlie Palmer,
Your name shall be sung forever,
Repeated, repeated.
A tribute to the deity,
A gem for eternity.
When the waves wash up on the shore,
They whisper your name,
For the pebbles,
The stones,
The earth to hear.
When the flowers push up,
They strive towards you.
When the sun shines down,
He does it to please you.
When the heavens open,
Just to cleanse you.
When all life erupts in chorus,
It shall be your name screamed for eternity,
For Heaven to hear,
For Earth to hear,
For all to hear.

Charlie Palmer (14)
Exeter School

The New-Old Testament

Sam Freeman, you are magical,
Every raindrop praises your name.
The sun rises from the hill,
To saturate where you stand in light.
The world spins due to your strength,
The fires roar with your presence.
The rocks grind together,
When your name is whispered.
The storms and floods flash
When your name is spoken.
When your name is yelled
The mountains of fire explode.
No one can match your greatness,
No one can match your skill,
Sam Freeman, you are immortal.

Sam Freeman (14)
Exeter School

Gary Clapson

Gary Clapson you are a legend in your own time,
You are the Sherman tank of World War II,
Your turrets blast people into the universe.
You are the designer of quality sports cars,
You are known all over the universe,
You bring the plagues of the world.
You are the crème de la crème,
Nothing can stop you.
You are the controller of the elements,
Your shine is the brightest people can see
For you are the god, Gary Clapson.

Gary Clapson (14)
Exeter School

Who Is Who?

Edwin Cawthron you are a god,
You are a whale,
You are big and powerful,
You are the best the world has seen,
You are a legend,
You will not die,
You control everything.
Everything is second best to you, even God,
No one will ever be as powerful as you.
You are la crème de la crème,
You created everything.
Edwin Cawthron you are god,
You are clever,
You are hard,
You are the person everyone looks up to,
You are the tips of the highest mountains,
You are invincible,
You can communicate with other galaxies,
Edwin Cawthron you are obviously the greatest.

Edwin Cawthron (14)
Exeter School

Special Girl

Special girl I see in my eyes,
Special girl I don't despise.
The love is flying through her hair,
Like the cold winter air.
As beautiful as a butterfly,
When I see her she makes me cry.
The love will stay with me,
Just wait, wait and see.

Sean Borland (11)
Great Torrington Community School

School!

I hate school,
Especially when it's raining,
We have PE today, second lesson.
I wish I could just stay in bed,
I don't want to go outside,
It speaks of thunder today,
I wish it could go away.
I don't know what else to say,
But I'm sure it will come to me,
Yesterday it was sunny but cold
And the sun was standing out bright
And bold.
Why me?
Why me?
Why does it have to happen to me?
My life is bouncy until . . .
You will have to wait and see!

Suzanne Nicholson (11)
Great Torrington Community School

What?

A bunny on a lawnmower,
A duck driving a tractor,
A kitten on a surfboard,
A dog crashed in his car,
A zebra teaching 30 kids
And pigs washing a house.

People being laughed at
And pointed at in the zoo!

What?

Charles Mill (12)
Great Torrington Community School

Punch, My Loving Companion

He's cute and cuddly like a teddy bear,
The cat would sit on him to make him move.
Punch he loved to play, he would sit on my bed,
He would sleep under the Christmas tree to guard the presents
Or he would lie with Toby.
When the corn was in the barn,
You could put him down and he would be gone,
Like now you see him, now you don't.
If he went in he would come with 2 or 3 rats
But sadly we lost him 5 years ago.

Deborah Tucker (11)
Great Torrington Community School

Food

Food is lovely,
Food is great,
I love food especially a grape.
Fruit is lovely,
Fruit is great,
I love food, there's no debate.

Tom Hunt (11)
Great Torrington Community School

School

School is boring,
I don't care,
Want to doodle,
Don't have time to spare
'Cause I'm getting eaten by a grizzly bear.

Charlie Banfield (11)
Great Torrington Community School

Batty Old Woman

I saw this woman yesterday,
She had no fashion sense at all.
Her hair looked like a mop
And a nose like a tennis ball.

She looked really psycho
With a bird's nest on her head.
Her face looked like a dried up trout
And her glasses were bright red.

If I'd stayed a moment longer,
I'd probably be dead,
Staring at that psycho woman
With a bird's nest on her head!

Tyler Pollard (11)
Great Torrington Community School

Monkeys

Monkeys swinging in the trees,
Monkeys looking straight at me,
Monkeys laughing 1, 2, 3,
Monkeys Sam, Lucy and Lee.

Monkeys jumping from tree to tree,
Be careful though they might nick your car keys,
Monkeys are very hairy
And sometimes very scary.

Monkeys swing in the tree,
Monkeys looking straight at me,
Monkeys laughing 1, 2, 3,
Monkeys Sam, Lucy and Lee.

Bonny Davies (12)
Great Torrington Community School

Daniel

Daniel is so big,
There's nowhere to sit in class.
There's nothing left in the bakeries
Because Daniel has been there first.
His favourite teacher is Miss Tiller,
Who he just adores,
He loves her dark chocolate curly hair.
Daniel is so stressy, no one dares to go near him,
He has brown hair
And he's shaped like a rhino.

Zac Sanders (11)
Great Torrington Community School

Rainy Days

Today I cannot be bothered
To do anything at all,
It's raining and it's wet,
Because the weatherman came to call.

It's stuffy and it's dull
And there isn't any fresh air,
I had to wait for the bus
And now I have wet hair!

Amy Toop (11)
Great Torrington Community School

My English Teacher

The teacher I have for English
Tells us she's the best.
She thinks she is so pretty,
But she's actually a mess.

Billie Tubb (12)
Great Torrington Community School

What Am I?

Flying through the sky,
Bump a cloud,
Bright red, so proud,
Win me, pop me, let me go,
Let me fly, I love it so
At the fair, I make lovers swoon,
What am I?

A balloon.

Fiona Nicholls (13)
Great Torrington Community School

Autumn!

After school
I collected some conkers,
It started to rain,
I stood by the window,
The grass was soggy
And the trees were bare.

I miss summer,
I wonder if it can hear me now.

Alex Gillespie (12)
Great Torrington Community School

Why?

Why is the question on everyone's lips?
Why is the beginning of every question?
Why is the answer for everything?
But why is why the answer and question?

Alex Keeley (12)
Great Torrington Community School

Nameless Poem

What shall I write?
  I'm just sitting here, thinking of what to do!
    Everybody else is writing,
      I can hear the scratching of their pens!

I'd better think of something!
  My teacher is scanning the tables
    For anyone not working,
      Anyone like *me!*

That evil eye has landed on me!
  Her short, stout legs are walking towards me!
    Her chubby hand reaches towards my work!
      Ar . . .

Leticia Kent (11)
Great Torrington Community School

Weather Feelings

The wind blows,
The rain falls,
It makes me feel low.

The clouds clear,
The sun shines,
It makes me feel fine.

Hailstones, snow and sleet
Gives me very cold hands and feet,
Hat and gloves keep me warm.

Thunder and lightning
Is very scary and frightening,
Flash, bang, very frightening.

Tom Gooch (11)
Great Torrington Community School

Autumn Days

Autumn days
    Heavy showers.

Autumn days
    Fading flowers.

Autumn days
    Falling leaves.

Autumn days
    Windswept trees.

Autumn days
    Frosty nights.

Autumn days
    Harvest delights.

David Andrew (11)
Great Torrington Community School

Why Oh Why?

Why oh why do I make my mum sigh?
My football boots are dirty,
My bedroom's a mess,
I've lost my school jumper - again.

Could this be why?

I've not done my homework,
I'm teasing my sister,
I've not gone to bed
And it's half-past nine.

Maybe I must try!

Sean Letheren (11)
Great Torrington Community School

Fruit

Oranges

I like oranges, the smell,
The tasty juice inside.
I like the nice round shape.
I think the colour is so groovy,
My mum loves oranges and so do I.

Bananas

I like bananas,
The smell is lovely,
The tasty soft centre.
Lots of monkeys like bananas
But I'm not a monkey.
Well I might be a bit cheeky!

Grapes

I love grapes,
They're my best fruit.
I love it when you pierce your teeth
Through the skin and juice squirts out.
I think I like grapes best 'cause wine
Is made out of them.

Siân Davies (11)
Great Torrington Community School

A Poem

The whirling, swirling darkness,
The multicoloured flashing lights,
A flash, darkness screaming,
Swallowed by the sound.
I don't like discos!

Lindsay McLeod (12)
Great Torrington Community School

What To Forget At School

Forget that two times four is eight,
Forget the name of every state,
Forget the answers to the test,
Forget which way is east or west.

Forget the myths from Ancient Rome,
Forget to bring your books from home,
Forget the words you learned to spell,
Forget to hear the break time bell.

Forget your teacher's name,
Forget the after school game,
Forget which team's supposed to win,
Forget to turn your homework in.

Forget the distance to the moon,
Forget how many days in June,
Forget the capital of France,
But don't forget to wear your pants.

Daniel Copp (11)
Great Torrington Community School

Road To Germany

England won last night 1-0,
Owen scored the goal.
Wales played last night as well,
I don't know what the score was.
Republic of Ireland played as well
Against the Faroe Islands.
Scotland are bottom of their group;
They've only 1 point
And England are top of their group;
They've got 10 points.

Ross Gallagher (11)
Great Torrington Community School

Safari Poem

On safari you ride around Africa
In a jeep with a guide you hired.
Then all the stuff he shows you gets boring
So you chuck him out
And give him a small tip.
You ride along
Trying to find more exciting animals
When suddenly
A monkey tries to jump on the windscreen.

Your mum and dad are wishing that they never
Threw out the guide
And that he would help them now.
They keep giving the monkey their crisps
But the monkey just wants more
And keeps on pestering them.
Suddenly the guide comes and pushes it away
And as he gets into the jeep again he says,
'I told you so.'

Hannah Jury (11)
Great Torrington Community School

Toilet Paper

Toilet paper and what people think of it,
Toilet paper it is so soft,
It never stays so clean,
You always have the dirty urge
To stain the padded sheet.

And then you drop it
And flush the chain,
Bye, bye you say again,
Your bum is clean, the paper's gone . . .
Phew and what a stench you've made.

James Mill (12)
Great Torrington Community School

Dinner - No More!

My neighbour's cat is very quiet,
She is black like midnight
With a topping of white vanilla ice cream.

She sneaks around on our garden wall.
If she smells you're cooking fish,
There will be no more fish for you.
So from now on I keep my eye on her
And then she won't pinch my dinner.

Jazmine Ker (11)
Great Torrington Community School

Boris

Boris toddles
As he tries to run to you,
He looks up at you
With his moonlit eyes.
Can you guess who he is?
Four legs,
Four weeks,
More than four memories.

Bethany Nancekivell (11)
Great Torrington Community School

On My Mind!

It gets on my mind,
When I don't know what to write
And when I think my candle goes out.
It's a pain,
It's a pain,
My brain goes bang, bang
All day long . . . !

Nicole Rous (12)
Great Torrington Community School

Chico

I think he's really cute,
Cuddly as a white fluffy cloud,
But it's annoying when he drops
A mud covered mangled tennis ball at my feet
When I'm trying to watch TV.

My sister was asleep on the sofa earlier
And he was watching over her,
Guarding her like an Alsatian at a safe,
He wouldn't hurt a fly
But he'll eat the occasional rabbit.

Aidan Barnes (11)
Great Torrington Community School

My Bus

I hate the bus today,
Everyone's on board
And everyone has to stand.
People throwing paper,
It falls to the floor.
I fall off the bus
Into a huge puddle.

Kieran Ford (11)
Great Torrington Community School

Going To School

I went to school today, it was raining cats and dogs,
There were acorns smashing into the windscreen.
Nearly at school now, get held up in some traffic lights,
So slow it is like a snail.

Stuart Allin (11)
Great Torrington Community School

Chickens

Sometimes when I'm in pain I run about
Like a headless chicken, I think they're mental ducks,
With a red ribbon on their heads,
Clucking and running around, looking for food and trouble.
I'm actually scared of chickens,
I hate it when they come up to you with no fear,
And then move their heads from side to side as if they are saying,
'What you doing here?'
As if you were some creature from a different planet.
Like myself!

Samuel Kinsella (11)
Great Torrington Community School

Cats

Cats are cute and cuddly,
I love seeing cats,
I adore their purr and the way they walk.
I like their way of looking all sweet and innocent,
I love to play with them.
I don't know why but they make me laugh,
When they jump up and down, trying to catch small flying bugs.
My brother and sisters have cats.
I really want a cute, cuddly, sweet, innocent cat.
I like ginger ones, tabby ones, tortoiseshell,
Fluffy ones and all types of cat!

Stephanie Garner (12)
Great Torrington Community School

Haiku

Summer is the best
You can sunbathe and have fun,
But now autumn's come.

Evie Page (11)
Great Torrington Community School

Pheasant

A pheasant playing with his friend,
A peaceful, calm bird,
Colourful and bright,
Oh but how thick.

They play happily,
Chasing each other around,
Suddenly they come across a road,
A lady pheasant on the other side.

Well a road and a pheasant not good,
One, two, three, fine so far,
Four, five, six *splat* . . .
Oh dear what was that?

Josh Hughes (12)
Great Torrington Community School

My Fruit Bowl

M y magical fruit bowl is always full,
Y ummy home-grown apples it holds within.

F reshly I peeled my orange as my stomach growled,
R ipping the pieces off and putting them into my mouth.
U nusually there is a pineapple, yum, yum I think,
I get out my spoon to eat my kiwi.
T ut, tut goes my dad as I spit out the watermelon pips.

B ananas, pears and grapes I eat with custard. 'Ergh,' says my sister.
O nly mangoes left so I'll make a chutney.
W ell it looks like I'll have to go shopping tomorrow.
L ovely, lovely fruit bowl never go away.

Eleanor Stacey (12)
Great Torrington Community School

Starry Night

The gold stars are so bright,
Shiny as a new penny
In the purse-like sky.

The clouds are so fluffy
Like cotton candy on a stick,
They float in the sky.

The moon is so light
In the starry pitch-black night
And you'll sleep at night.

Jessica Blythe (12)
Great Torrington Community School

The Twit Of All Twits!

My brother is a twit,
I hate him, a lot!
All he ever does is moan
And whinge and shout,
And locks himself in his bedroom!
He's like a little creature,
He just sneaks down for tea,
If you're lucky!

Alex Bluck (11)
Great Torrington Community School

Cars Haiku

Ferrari and Porsche
Lamborghini and Bentley
One day will be mine.

Jack Gilbert (11)
Great Torrington Community School

Stars

Shining, sparkling, shiny stars,
Yellow like bananas.
It gleams, it gleams behind those bars,
It's swift throughout the sky,
It's ancient, silent and secret.
Up in the sky, way up high, beyond any dream
Where no one has been.
To some people it's a big mystery.
Others think they're millions of years old.
It must be cold.
I look upon a Saturday night
With no care in sight,
They fly like a kite,
Trying so hard to be bright,
It just sets the sky alight.

Daniel Simpson (11)
Great Torrington Community School

At Night

Trees turn to giants,
Creatures turn to monsters,
Believe me I've seen it
And in the morning it's just a memory.
Giants turn into dead shadows,
Monsters destroy everything in sight
And then silence . . .
At dawn
The sun rises up,
The man in the moon fades down,
The giants turn to trees,
The monsters turn to creatures.

Miriam Kimber (11)
Great Torrington Community School

What Is It?

A snap of a twig, what is it?
A rustle in the bushes, what is it?
A swishing noise like a tail but what is it?
A shadow between the trees, what is it?
A pair of eyes between the grass, what is it?
A spotted tail, what is it?
A spotted tail, ears and eyes, what is it?
A short patch of grass, I see a spotted back, what is it?
A spotted tail, back, ears, eyes and . . .
A whole head with a huge nose sniffing me out,
What is it?

  L ion!
  U rrrr,
  N o!
  C heetah!
  H elp!

Tasmin Bidgway (11)
Great Torrington Community School

School

I hate school today,
It's damp and wet in class,
When I got out of class, the grass was wet
But the sun came out
But then it was time to go.

Josh Day (11)
Great Torrington Community School

Football Fantasy

Whenever you play football
It hits you in the head,
No one else,
Just you instead.

Samantha Bond (12)
Great Torrington Community School

Surfed Out

Billowing masses of foam crashing elegantly
Like dancing horses.

The low grumble of the sea sends tingles up my spine.

Board in hand I race towards the water.

The icy ripple of the liquid between my toes.

Paddling out, my arms ache with anticipation
For the perfect wave.

Here it comes,
The thunderous roar of the enormous wall of water.

The surface sparkles with diamond sheen as
I prepare to ride the wave of my dream.

The barrelling tube rushes over my head.

I've done it,
I run to shore, all my fears left behind.

Owen Ward (12)
Great Torrington Community School

Snakes

Sneaky snakes
Slither through
Slippery places.

Snakes are cautious
In what they do.

They spend all day
Just slithering around.

How boring can it be?

Emma Edgecombe (11)
Great Torrington Community School

Haiku

My mum is so
Cool, mental, super,
That's my mum.

My mum likes
Cooking for me tonight,
That's my mum.

My mum hates
Messy bedrooms,
That's my mum.

My mum will
Shout and yell,
That's my mum.

My mum gets
Road rage, yep,
I love my mum.

William Bennett (11)
Great Torrington Community School

My Estate

Our estate is very loud
Especially in summer.
Some nights when people go to bed
Children are messing about,
Shouting loud
Under the black sky.

Under the blue moon
Children party like baboons,
My lovely estate.

Teresa Beakhouse (11)
Great Torrington Community School

The Monster Behind

Its cold drawing breath ruffles my matted hair,
I'm too frightened to turn around, I keep on walking,
Step by fearful step I go,
It snorts, as if to let me know it's there,
I resist the urge to look behind me,
It lets out a cry, a cry for help?
No, it is about to pounce,
That's why it's wailing so terribly.
A hand reaches out and grabs my shoulders,
Making it impossible for me to carry on,
This was the part I was dreading,
I was to face the creature . . .
I opened my mouth, ready to scream,
But closed it again quickly,
A wave of relief gushed over me,
'You alright sis?'

Lydia Fallaize (12)
Great Torrington Community School

As I Sit

In the wind as the
Trees sway at their own pace
I sit and think.

At night as the stars start
To shine, I wonder what it
Would be like to be so high.

As moon shines through
The trees, the hawk uses
The light to swoop to its prey.

Sam Nicholls (11)
Great Torrington Community School

My Dog

My dog liked cat food,
Any would do,
She was funny and energetic,
She was like a kangaroo.

She had brown eyes,
Like tree trunks,
She was very protective,
And she loved her shepherd's pie.

She had a black coat,
She liked my cat,
She would never bite,
Or chew shoes or hats.

This dog was the best,
She was very playful,
She had a loud bark,
But now she's gone.

Jade Courtney (12)
Great Torrington Community School

My House

My house is massive,
There are 25 acres of grounds,
I have a swimming pool.
In November, December, January,
February and March it is very quiet,
But in the summer it is very busy,
I have lots of friends to play with.
It is as old as the Doomsday book.

Ben Harper (11)
Great Torrington Community School

My Little Sister

My little sister drives me up the wall,
My little sister always wants to play ball,
Me and my sister always fight,
My little sister shouts all night,
My little sister always thinks she's right,
My little sister scratched my bike,
My little sister is the best,
Even though she is a pest.

Seraphina Plows (12)
Great Torrington Community School

A Question

Here's a question, can you guess
What this tailed creature might be?
She purrs like a chainsaw,
She plops like a pig,
But here you go,
She's my dude,
Just black and white,
Plain, ploppy, purring.

Bryony Porter (11)
Great Torrington Community School

Black

Black . . . it's under stones,
Hidden away from the sun.
Black is nothingness, a blank void.
Black calls evil from the four corners of this Earth.
Black is what you see in the dark of
Night looking into the black of space.
Black.

Samuel Thorp (11)
Great Torrington Community School

Tammy

My gran's cat Tammy is a tortoiseshell,
Creeps around like a cheetah,
Shy as a shrimp on the seashore,
She runs around the house.
Lies on her back and rolls like a roller coaster,
As soft as a velvet cushion,
Sees in the dark with piercing sharp eyes,
Curls up in a ball on the bed,
Keeping Gran's feet warm and cosy.

Hannah Parkinson (11)
Great Torrington Community School

The Sky Is Blue

The sky is blue,
Not red, pink or purple,
It goes black when it's late at night!
The clouds it has are normally white . . .
But when it's raining,
They're black, a nasty dull grey!

Matthew Waterson (11)
Great Torrington Community School

Sun - Haiku

It is always hot
My family play all day
You get very bored.

Eloise Loufer (11)
Great Torrington Community School

Roses Are . . .

Roses are red,
Violets are blue,
I hate boys,
And they hate me too,
I've had a boyfriend
I don't want anymore,
Boys are icky!

Roses are red,
Violets are blue,
Boys can't spell,
I can't too,
Boys smell horribly sickly!

Roses are red,
Violets are blue,
Who invented boys,
They're worse than my sister's toys!
Boys wear too much smelly stuff!

Roses are red,
Violets are blue,
Boys are a waste of time,
Girls are too!
Boys are too loud!

Roses are red,
Violets are blue,
I can't stand love,
How can you?
Boys take ages with their hair!

Roses are red,
Violets are blue,
I've got a new boyfriend,
My friend has too,
Boys are OK!

Roses are red,
Violets are blue,
Boys are alright,
Girls can be too,
I've got a boyfriend,
He's really nice,
Boys are fine!

Rae Cornwall (11)
Great Torrington Community School

Sky

The sky is blue,
With a bright yellow sun,
No clouds in sight,
Except for one,
Tiny black specks flying around,
Little birds all of one kind,
The sun is shiny and bright,
And then it just goes
But where?

Claire Sanders (11)
Great Torrington Community School

The Pickled Smelling Person

The pillow got pulled off by the pickled smelling person,
The pickled smelling person pulled the pencil in half,
The pickled smelling person liked pickled onion plaster,
People repel off the pickled smelling person,
The pickled smelling person is sad because
No one goes near him.

Jacob Niklasson (11)
Great Torrington Community School

My Illusion

Waves sweep back and forth,
Palm trees sway in the soft breeze,
The sun tans my body
As I lay there
On the hot sand.

I open my eyes,
Trees fight the wind,
The clouds hide the sun,
I sit there cold,
Wrapping my arms around myself.

Krystina Heistercamp (11)
Great Torrington Community School

My Puppy

I have a new puppy, she's brown and white,
And when you play with her, she likes to nip and bite,
She's not very obedient when you ask her to sit and stay,
All she wants to do is run away and play.
She can't go for her walkies yet, she hasn't had all her jabs,
But when she's a bit older, we'll take her out with her dad,
When it's night-time and she's tucked in her bed, so cute and sweet,
It's a blessing in disguise as she's no longer under my feet.

Stacey-Ella Freemantle (12)
Great Torrington Community School

The Apple

The apple is red and is shining,
And even sometimes you
Can see a red face,
It is like someone is
Trapped inside a red bubble.

The apple sparkles in the day.

Philippe Pauchet (12)
Great Torrington Community School

Making Models

I like building models,
Especially with my dad.
It takes a long time but in the end
It's worth it because it is special
Because we did it together.
On days like Sundays, I like to get a model out
And build all day,
I just think making models is fun
Because once it's done and built,
It's good fun to play and
I enjoy making them.

Daniel Stubbs
Great Torrington Community School

Snake

As the snake slithers through the grass,
His tail following its head,
He looks rather hungry,
Making his way back to his bed,
His skin is rather scaly,
His tongue is rather long,
But wait till you watch him catch his prey,
It doesn't take that long.

Natalie Day (12)
Great Torrington Community School

Henry - Haiku

Henry is the best
He is better than the rest
He has passed the test.

Elliot Brant (12)
Great Torrington Community School

Home

Rain drops down my face,
As I run in the wet rain,
I wish I was home.

All I see is rain,
Not sunny just plain, wet rain,
I wish I was home.

The sky is darker,
With wind blowing on my face,
I wish I was home.

David Quinn (11)
Great Torrington Community School

Budgies

They are as chirpy as a whistle,
Budgies budge by each other,
They go 'cheep'
When you whistle at them they
Whistle back to you,
Mattie, Charlie, James and Mia.

They peck at their seed all day long,
Cheep, cheep!

Kathryn Masterson (12)
Great Torrington Community School

Food

Food is great,
On my plate,
It's so yummy,
In my tummy,
I could eat all day,
Especially today,
Food is great.

Kimberley Harding (12)
Great Torrington Community School

Westies

W inter white
E yes, dark and bright
S mall and cute
T ough and astute.

H ealthy and happy
I ntelligent puppy
G uarding and keeping our
H ome from weeping
L oyal companion
A human's best friend
N oting our tone
D igs for her bone

T iny terminator
E dging to go
R unning the chase
R eaching the place
I n and stands
E verything still
R ight to *sleep*!

Adam Bewes (12)
Great Torrington Community School

Tree

It starts as a small seed,
Grows as big as the sky,
It's green like grass,
Brown like chocolate.

When the clouds go dark and
Rain pours from the sky,
It grows really big,
When winter comes, it loses its green
And goes brown,
When spring comes back
It comes back again green.

Megan Avery (11)
Great Torrington Community School

That's British Weather For You

In Europe the summer comes,
Not one cloud in sight,
With the dazzling sun gleaming,
Unfortunately for tourists in Britain,
One too many clouds,
Some rain now and then,
That's British weather for you.
When you look out of the window,
And you see the pouring rain,
You wish it was summer,
Sometimes you'd like to splash in all the puddles,
Sometimes you'd like to just sit and watch it,
That's British weather for you.

Ruby Heywood (12)
Great Torrington Community School

Barney

I am writing a poem about my former dog,
Well technically he is ours but
My sister takes care of him,
He is 3 (in dog years that is 21)
His coat is an ivory, white colour,
His eyes are giant,
When you look into them, you feel like,
You have just fallen into a deep, dark, dark hole
In complete dark brown surrounding you,
He was a small dog,
I remember when I came home from school
He used to greet me frantically . . .
'Yep' I remember the good days.

Josh Jones (11)
Great Torrington Community School

The Star Swimmer!

I'm at the pool,
Paying to go in,
Waiting for my ticket,
So they can let me swim.

Into the changing room,
Rush behind the door,
Changing into my cossie,
Changing's just a chore.

I see the clear blue water,
I can't wait to get in,
I do a big, fat belly flop,
And *slap* I am in!

Swimming, diving, splashing, laughing,
With family and friends,
We're the nosiest people in the pool,
Until our session ends.

Out we get and rush to dry,
Oh no, it's time to go,
I get changed and do my hair,
I'm always very slow.

Everyone has to wait for me,
Then back off to the car,
They all boast off their swimming skills,
But really I'm the star!

Katie Mills (12)
Great Torrington Community School

Oh What To Do In This Dingy English Classroom!

Thrust into this dingy classroom
We die like lampless moths
Locked into the desolation of
Fluorescent lights and metal desks.

Ten minutes until the bell rings
What use are commas and exclamations
To us in our daily lives?
Can we use it to unlock the secrets,
Of our universe?

Five minutes until the bell rings
Cruel English teacher,
Won't you let us go?

Oh what to do during English
The possibilities are limitless,
There's drawing and yawning,
And portable chess.
There's dozing and dreaming
And feeling confused.
There's humming and strumming,
And looking bemused,
You can stare at the clock,
You hum a little song,
I've tried just about everything,
To pass the time along.

Bryony Peachey (12)
Great Torrington Community School

Running The Race

All I can see
Is the track right in front of me,
The red of the tarmac,
The white of the lines,
Are there people in front of me?
People behind?
All I must do is get to the line.
The rhythm of my feet,
The swinging of my arms,
Essential is the co-ordination,
                    The determination.
In my fight
To get to
The line.

Jemimah Lane (13)
Great Torrington Community School

Shhh, Shhh

'Shhh, shhh,'
Whispers the wind,
'Follow me, follow me,'
Beckon the trees,
'I'll soothe your aching eyes,
Your aching eyes,'
Gurgles the stream,
'And I'll lead you home,
Lead you home,'
Mutters the moon,
As you slip into peaceful oblivion.

Yasmin Clarke-Collins (13)
Great Torrington Community School

Hallowe'en

Hallowe'en, Hallowe'en,
A time to dress up and play,
The witches and vampires,
Scare people away,
With them all dressed
In black, they give you a fright,
And the pumpkins that
Give off a glowing bright light.

Hallowe'en, Hallowe'en,
A time to trick or treat,
For people so kind to
Give you a sweet,
It's all so much fun,
To be out at night,
So be aware,
Hallowe'en will soon
Be here.

Kirsty Spear (12)
Great Torrington Community School

My Little Sister . . .

She's sometimes sweet,
She's sometimes horrid,
But she's a cool little sister.

She can be nice,
She can be nasty,
But she's my cheeky little sister.

She pulls my hair,
I pull hers back,
But I love my little sister.

Jessica Matthews (13)
Great Torrington Community School

Seabird: Skyking

Come escape the hype,
To a secret life,
Where troubles disappear,
A seabird's world,
Will soon be unfurled,
And happiness will be sheer.

Come fly further,
To a quaint harbour,
Where fishermen's homes lie,
Let us sit on masts,
On boats of the past,
Then take off to the sky.

Come fly with me,
To an unknown sea,
Where no man can be found,
Then dip our talons,
In the ocean's fathoms,
And skykings we shall be crowned.

Megan Chesters (13)
Great Torrington Community School

Ahoy There Sailor

'Ahoy there sailor,' the young man said,
'What's that on your head?'

'Ahoy there sailor,' the young man said,
'You have got to get that dog fed.'

'Ahoy there sailor,' the young man said,
'I've taken a nasty bash to my head.'

'Ahoy there sailor,' the young man said,
'I can't carry on, I'm nearly dead!'

Kelvin Lancaster (12)
Great Torrington Community School

Our World

Blood, tears and painful threats
Fill the air and suffocate.
The only thing that can breathe
Are those so pure and those that grieve.

War, pain and hateful words
Kill things of beauty, trees and birds,
Consequences of bad words,
Killing our world, packed and sold.

The ground beneath us soon will fall
But all we do is stand up tall,
It's now too late to change the past,
But history repeats and is repeating fast.

Countries just can't realise how
Quick they'll shrivel up and die.
Love is lost and friends will fade,
If our world is not remade.

A new start is what we need
To make our world fresh, always clean
Then add love and charity
Then our world is fit to be seen.

Toni Alexander (13)
Great Torrington Community School

Poem Feelings

Poems make me cry,
Poems make me smile,
Poems make me sad,
Poems make me sing,
Poems make me quiet,
Poems make me stick like glue.

Karl Knight (12)
Great Torrington Community School

Fire

Fire is dangerous but beautiful,
Golden sparks fly here and there,
Across the long burnt grass.
Big amber flames, red hot, roar into,
The silent night.
The warmth is tingling, it makes
You relaxed and sleepy.

As I sit here on a mossy log,
My eyes are mesmerised by the fire,
So many colours bright and vibrant,
I think how this wonderful thing can kill,
Burn and melt, leaving devastation behind it
When fire is out of control.

Lauren Priest (13)
Great Torrington Community School

Desert Sun

Sun beams down,
Skin goes red,
Very quickly burns my head,
Skin is peeling, falling down,
My feet are blistering on the red hot ground,
As my lips begin to crack,
I start to see that water lacks,
Head is spinning all around,
Face hits the desert ground,
I hear something, a sound, a rattlesnake,
Sliding across the ground!

Sian Bartlett (12)
Great Torrington Community School

Anger

A fizzing lava floods your veins,
A cauldron of hate is your brain,
Clenching fists
A flaming soul
Against you everyone scores a goal.
A frowning head,
A screaming heart,
Everyone has learnt your art,
A vengeful heart full of hate,
Your line of life never straight.
A surging hell carries you on
All you hear is a solitary song.

Annie Ritson (12)
Great Torrington Community School

Jimbo

There once was a boy called Jimbo,
Who's girlfriend was a bit of a bimbo,
He thought she was nice,
Till she picked up a knife,
Now it's easy to limbo!

He lost three inches,
And his girlfriend pinches,
She thumped him,
Then dumped him,
Now he's down in the dumps
And his little bald head
Is covered in lumps!

Luke Daniel (12)
Great Torrington Community School

Just Like The Others

Turn on
the lamp

Lifting up the
flap,

Going into the
camp,

Lay down for a
nap,

And pulled up
the covers,

Just like the
others.

Then I woke
up,

Put on the cap,

Lifting the flap,

Went out with
the pups,

To give them a
walk,

And had a talk,

Just like the
others.

Amy Crocker (12)
Great Torrington Community School

My Chinchilla

I had a chinchilla,
Her name was Cilla,
She was very sweet,
But had awful big feet.

Oh Cilla, Cilla my
Fluffy chinchilla.

She bit into my top,
That I brought from the shop,
Oh my white chinchilla,
I wanted to kill 'er!

Oh Cilla, Cilla my
Fluffy chinchilla.

Charlotte Jeffery (12)
Great Torrington Community School

Tractors

A bright orange tractor gleaming in the sun,
Along came another one and
He said to the other one,
'Come on chum,'
So they went out ploughing,
One Sunday afternoon,
And when their work was done,
They said, 'Tudalu.'

Matthew Webber (12)
Great Torrington Community School

The Soldier

When he gets to Heaven,
To St Peter he will tell -
'One more soldier reporting Sir,
I've served my time in Hell.'

Joshua Goaman (12)
Great Torrington Community School

Time

It can't walk,
It can't fly,
But it runs away,
And flashes by.

Numerals and digits,
Tiredness and fidgets,
Ticking and chiming,
Two arms miming.

Blyth Bosher (12)
Great Torrington Community School

Special

Can you make me feel special?
Will you show me you care?
Will you speak with kind words,
And ruffle my hair?
I need your encouragement,
To blossom and grow,
Can you make me feel special?
I just need to know.

James Fishleigh (12)
Great Torrington Community School

Flower

F lowers are beautiful
L ovely and bright
O pen in the sunshine light
W et or dry, they still make us smile
E ven in death, the coffin they cover
R eminding us all, the loss of a lover.

Owen Dell (12)
Great Torrington Community School

Winter

The leaves have changed colour,
And are falling off the trees,
The nights are getting shorter,
The streams begin to freeze.

Soon the snow is coming,
A blanket will cover the land,
It will be as though you're on a beach,
Covered in luscious sands.

And now the winter comes to an end,
Christmas and New Year pass,
New things to do, new people to meet,
Oh life is such a blast.

Billy Curtis (12)
Great Torrington Community School

The Fix

I stand in the sand,
The wind whips my hair and the salt stings my eyes,
I feel a sudden urge and grab my stick,
I dive in the ocean breakers, really paddling hard,
I'm up, I swerve, really pounding my rails,
But no, I dig my rails too hard!
And I'm down,
And as I breathe in the salty air,
I don't care, I've had my fix.

Lauren Slater (12)
Great Torrington Community School

Fear

Silence falls over the children scattering through
                                      the haunted house,
Darkness was everywhere except for the children's eyes,
Black cats everywhere to be seen,
Hearts pounding as they tiptoed through the dusty kitchen,
Goosebumps appearing all over them as they
Creep up the wooden staircase,
Terrified to find someone living there.

Lydia Singer (11)
Grenville College

Fear

Silence is broken by the hoot of an owl,
Darkness surrounds me on a ghostly night,
Black blinds my eyes with silky fingers,
My heart is thudding wildly,
Cold shivers creep down my back,
Goosebumps crawl onto my shivering skin,
Terrifying noises tiptoe into my ears,
Frightening night, the worst of my fears.

Rebekah Locke (11)
Grenville College

Fear

Silence is deafening,
Darkness fills the room,
Black, shadows light,
Heart is frozen,
Cold wraps around you,
Goosebumps cover your skin,
Fear is empty.

Tom Marsden (11)
Grenville College

Fear

Silence was spreading around the spooky house,
Darkness creeping into every corner and gap,
Black air filled with layers of dust,
Heart pounding with fear,
Cold was reaching me and shivering down my spine,
Goosebumps sprouted up from underneath my skin,
Floorboards creaking as I tremble with fear,
Strange noises coming from above and under me,
Trembling as I look around,
Chills spiralling down my freezing spine,
Quivers when I see and feel something bony,
Scared as I waddled up the splintered stairs,
Worried I might be seen by ghosts,
Skeleton bones scattered endlessly up the corridors,
Suddenly, a loud *bang!*
I run downstairs tripping at the bottom,
Slam the big black doors behind me,
Cold, trembling body.

William Shortridge (11)
Grenville College

Fear

Silence was not usual around here . . .
Darkness had swept over quickly . . .
Black was everywhere around me . . .
Heart was thumping like a hammer . . .
Goosebumps were trembling all around me . . .
Cold had tingled down my spine . . .
The dusty street was windy and bits of paper and
Twigs blew in my face,
I decided to sprint back to my house and stay there
Safe till morning.

Chloe MacGillivray (11)
Grenville College

Fear

Silence fell over the haunted mansion except for
The creaking of dusty floorboards and the tick tock
Of the old grandfather clock.
Darkness was all around me, I was terrified,
Black figures were walking around outside and
I suddenly got chills down my spine.
My heart was pounding, I was quivering under my pillow,
Goosebumps were popping up all over my body,
I was freezing,
I started hearing strange noises all around me,
I began to tremble,
Cold shivers ran all over my body.
I was terrified.

Daniel Rogerson (11)
Grenville College

Fear!

Silence was broken by the howling of the wind,
Darkness filled the air,
Black was everywhere you looked,
My heart was thumping like a bomb about to explode,
Cold shivers went up my spine,
Goosebumps covered my frozen legs,
Noises came from every corner,
Dust choked you as you wandered,
Trembling like jelly I sprint to the door,
I feel like I am pushing on a brick wall,
Eventually the door opens with a loud squeak.

Georgina Barrington (11)
Grenville College

Lydford Gorge

Crunchy looking lychen,
So soft and so smooth,
Brightly covered water,
Small dark cave.

Autumn is here,
The leaves are raining from the sky,
The beams of light of Heaven opening,
The devilish black fish that swim from Hell.

Water gushing down the rocks,
Making a coshuhhh noise,
A tree with millions of holes,
From a woodpecker.

Lydford Gorge is a place of scenery,
From banks of mud to rocks and water,
If you want to see these things I've said,
Go there, go there, go and see!

Oliver White (12)
Grenville College

Fear!

Silence is a golden attic,
Darkness impales me,
Black shadows coming towards me,
Heart thumping, scared out of my wits,
Coldness all around me, it's just like a dream,
Goosebumps down my back,
Terrified, is what I am,
Strange noises are coming from that corner,
I freeze, the only thing to do is climb back down the ladder,
Never to come back to the dusty attic.

Jonathan Brookes (11)
Grenville College

The Waterfall

Lydford forest is a beautiful place,
The river Lyd gently flowing,
And the soft breeze blowing,
With the autumn leaves dropping like paper.

The rocks are thick with slime,
Nearby lay traces of moles,
Upturned earth from badger holes,
Little dormouse tubes on trees.

The river began to meander through rocks,
Then it crashed at a tremendous pace,
Down it went off the rock face,
When it landed, it fizzed and popped.

The bubbles floated around in the current,
The water was whirling,
Spinning around and round swirling,
Then it floated downstream.

Ebony Gunn (12)
Grenville College

Lydford Gorge

Canopies of the trees dangled over me,
Leaves tumbled down,
Rotten trees were skeletons,
The forest whispered,
Shadows of the trees danced.

Amazing roaring waterfall,
Niagara Falls,
Mythical giant's tear,
Smashing glasses,
A clash of thunder.

Sarah Hookway (13)
Grenville College

Just A Dream

Screams shriek down the chimney
Ashes scattering everywhere
Shadows moving, creeping
I open my eyes, it's not a dream
I didn't open the window
It's cold

The colour drained from her face
As the shadows still remained at the door
The shadows black, cold, silent
The windows shut
He's coming closer
She'd heard tales, never thought true

It was a dream
It was a dream
It had to be
In her dream she didn't wake up
But that was just a dream
It had to be
She never woke up
She was burned
And her ashes shrieked through the chimney
It wasn't just a dream.

Rachel Wingate (13)
Grenville College

Fear

Silence falls around the house,
Darkness is all around us,
Black as black is all you can see,
Hearts are pounding with terror and fright,
Cold as ice is all in the air,
Goosebumps are crawling over our bodies,
Spooked as ever in the night,
Strange noises broke the terrible silence.

James Guilfoyle (12)
Grenville College

The Clumsy Elephant

The clumsy elephant walks down the street knocking everything over,
With such size, weight and beauty all in one,
But still with such clumsiness
He holds his head up high despite such looks of filth and disgust.

He is the one who was here first, and he knows and shows that
He is the one that in one giant footstep could crush anyone of us
He is the one who can spit water with the force and velocity
Of a fire hose
He looks down on us as we would look down on an ant.

From such ancient times and from ancient ancestors
He is the one with the wisdom and knowledge
He has seen families die and has had to leave dying relatives
Just so that life can be spared from malicious poachers
That want his beauty.

He may be clumsy but with such pride what does it matter?

Lyndon Wake (14)
Grenville College

Clown

His eyebrows are two strips of cotton wool,
His nose is a big, red cherry,
A sticky-out chin like a tree's knot,
His hair like red springs, appearing everywhere,
His big, clumsy shoes are like those squiggle, oval balloons.
His trousers are sleeping bags,
And his shirt is like a leopard's spots.
His false smile is like a crescent moon,
Waiting to give off a huge beam of light.

Joanna Lock (13)
Grenville College

The White Devil

The river whooshing, whirling, swirling,
Charging frantically down the valley,
I wonder how long it has been running,
Over the cliff face, the water does soar.

This amazing never-ending water source,
Sluicing through the rocks with such force,
How many generations have bathed in this amazing river?
How many weary travellers have cooled their feet and
                               quenched their thirst?
All these questions remain unanswered.

The white lady plummets down, down and crash,
The incandescent spray soaks us all,
The Devil's cauldron a swirling whirlpool,
Want to go for a swim . . .
No! Watch out if you don't want to fall!

Holly Rampling (12)
Grenville College

Spring

Spring is here,
Winter's finished,
Lambs and chicks are being born,
A sign of new life.

The snowdrops are dying,
They've come to their end,
But, it's the daffodils prime time,
They're peeking their heads out.

The brightly coloured leaves,
Holding on the big old oak tree,
It's forming new buds,
To make baby oak trees.

Vicki Withecombe (13)
Grenville College

Him

Beautiful iridescent feather fell . . .
Landed gently at my feet . . .
I hardly noticed.
Too transfixed was I
He seemed to glow in front of me,
Terrifying.
This creature could destroy me in a flash
But here he stood beside me
But hardly tame
His skin did glow like snow when sun is shining.
This is a dream I thought,
This cannot be
This is not real
He gently shook his head.

With longing in his face
A mournful smile he smiled at me
And heavy hand did fall upon my shoulder.

His hands were cold,
Not like flesh of man.

Although I understood his message,
To you I cannot it relate,
It passed from him to me
No words, no thought, just knowing.

Please don't go,
My panic rose,
He placed a perfect finger upon a perfect lip
And smiled with warmth of summer day,
I knew then what his purpose was.

I will not leave you
Ever.

Eleanor Briggs (13)
Grenville College

Hell Of War

'Get up, get up, come on lads, let's go,'
Cried General Macally knee deep in the mud.
'The Germans are coming, come on lads get ready,'
The struggle for rifles and bullets begins.

The shells come down wailing,
The men are all screaming,
Then 'over the top'
And all hell breaks loose.

Every time we go over it's never the same,
Different craters and bodies all strewn on the floor.
Men groaning and moaning, and crying and dying,
And knowing that they have seen their last day.

Those that survive crawl back to their trenches
Coughing and hurting and mentally scared,
Then General Macally comes out of his quarters,
And says, 'Well done men, *we* really showed them.'

Then day turns to night,
But then at first light,
The chain of events start to happen again,
Like a bad roller coaster you just wish would end.

So do not be fooled and believe all the lies,
And the propaganda of war,
It's an honour to fight, ha ha yeah right,
You'll be dead with your face on the floor.

Michelle Dymond (13)
Grenville College

Space

Space is dark and endless,
It's empty, no one about,
Just planets and further galaxies,
Some of which are way out of sight.

We watch the planets through a telescope,
There's Pluto and Neptune, Mercury and Mars,
All that way up near the stars,
All surrounded by nothingness.

The universe is extremely vast,
With comets and meteors flying everywhere,
There's space stations with the latest technology,
And satellites telling us about the latest news.

Space is so big,
There's so much more to see,
Maybe in the future we'll have better technology,
And maybe even later we'll be on Mars.

Nicholas Deakes (13)
Grenville College

Tennis

Tennis is a great game,
You hit a ball and it flies away.

It makes me feel great,
When I make a break.

But sometimes
I say to myself
'Hit that tennis ball right'
Before it falls.

My coach makes sure
That I don't hit the net,
So I can believe in myself,
To win the set.

Mark Murgelas (13)
Grenville College

Lydford Gorge

Stunning, beautiful is Lydford Gorge,
Rushing, raging the river bores.

Twisted shadows the tall trees cast,
Beside the river flowing fast.

Colourful toadstools dotted around,
Thriving on the soft, moist ground.

Floating gracefully the clouds lie low,
The tall flowers smoothly, slowly flow.

The sun illuminates the trees with light,
Making such a spectacular sight.

Furry squirrels dart and dash,
Beside the land and river clash.

The sun begins to set and now,
The waking dormouse, badgers and owls.

Start to rustle, scratch and shake,
As the light begins to break.

The darkness starts to shroud and weave,
Just as we pack up and leave.

Joshua Minici (12)
Grenville College

The Creature

It lives in the woods or in fields
There are different types of these
It makes its home out of wood
Or even under the ground.
They are employees of the Queen
It acts like a mole burrowing down
Its royalty is very useful and makes busy colonies
It is like a termite
They are like atoms.

Harry Swannack (12)
Grenville College

The River Lyd

On the trees the fungi are like spots,
The woodpecker has left little dots,
As the only clue that he exists.

The floor is covered in a dappled shade,
And the set of a badger, proudly made,
Is like a pile of sieved flour.

The river falls, tumbles and whirls,
As falling leaves gently swirl
Into the water.

Occasionally, a small brown trout,
Shoots and darts in and out
From under the rocks.

As the river smoothly bubbles
Over rocks, it troubles,
Tiny twigs clinging to the banks.

A white ribbon streams,
Down rocks that gleam,
In the sunlight.

Emma Corrick (12)
Grenville College

Who Am I?

Lightly trodden steps like an angel bound to earth,
Eyes like a cat about to pounce,
Nose like a dog, sniffing its path
And ears like a horse, twitching and alert.
The fluffed out tail of a well used paintbrush,
Swift as a cheetah on the hunt.
It goes through the day in a graceful way,
With a flaming coat of red.

Answer: A Fox

Nicolle Hockin (12)
Grenville College

The Coming Of Winter

The coming of winter,
The nights are drawing in,
The days becoming shorter,
The pattern doesn't alter.

Year after year it's always the same,
With the cold and the rain,
And the wind whistling by,
On grassy banks snowdrops lie.

The moon is shining brightly,
And the frost starts to glisten,
The house casts a glow,
While it begins to snow.

There's fun to be had,
Playing in the snow,
With snowmen to make,
And snowballs to throw.

But after all the darkness,
The light begins to show,
And I look to the spring,
With the warmth it will bring.

Aaron Penn (13)
Grenville College

The Ballerina

She is a graceful spinning top, constantly revolving,
Her delicate cobwebbed tutu lies flat.
Her long flamingo legs stand proud,
Leaning to her ribbon wrapped, nimble needle feet.
Her carefully placed netted bun perches on her smooth strands of silk.
Her intense glistening marble eyes hover over her pillar box mouth.

Abigail Taylor (12)
Grenville College

Lydford Gorge

There is a place of hidden secrets
In the woods of Lydford Gorge,
Where streams flow and combine
To come down as one great waterfall
That plummets from unseen heights.

Its graceful movement enchants you,
But behind the soft cover is a raging giant.
A thing of menace thrashing and racing,
Pounding and carving the rocks below.

It bubbles and froths like boiling water,
But calms and runs away into the woods.
Twisting and winding around the bedraggled trees,
It digs away at the muddy banks
And smoothes the rocky walls that lie in its way.

Triumphantly breaking out of the woods
To begin a new mysterious journey,
That will take it far away
From the woods of Lydford Gorge.

Sam Petty (12)
Grenville College

The Seasick Man

His face a green apple,
That wants to be peachy.

His body the shape of a 7,
Leaning over a bar that wants to be off this boat.

His T-shirt like mash potato from being sick,
He looks at the sea and thinks it is green.

His eyes like shrivelled up snails, watering like mad,
His mouth like a puffer fish waiting for the next blow.

When in the port he is happy
Off his worst nightmare.

Charlotte Handley (12)
Grenville College

Leaves

It starts its journey, detaching from a branch
Floating through the air, it catches the breeze.
It glides like a plane, surfing through the air
It falls down, down, down until thud. It hits the ground.

Without a sound it spins and tumbles,
Around the leaf covered ground.
Its journey has ended, but another has begun
The journey of being decomposed.

It rots until soggy and makes a mess all over the floor,
The colour has changed from healthy green
To dead brown.

After a while it is covered,
Its worst enemy, the rake, has come to sweep it away.
The leaf tries to resist but then gives in
And is flung onto the compost heap

Whilst there it wonders what the smell is
But never realises that it's itself
The journey has ended; it is flung off the heap
To emerge only as compost for the tulips.

The journey has ended but another leaf's has just begun.

Samuel Smith (13)
Grenville College

A Person

He sleeps in a cot,
His eyes are buttons,
His mouth is stitched closed,
His soft body is stuffed,
He makes me feel safe,
The fur on his chest is brown,
Grown up children play with him.

George Snell (12)
Grenville College

Make-Believe World

People whizzing around her,
Intent on carrying on with their self-contained lives,
But she's standing there lost and staring at it all,
Not sure how to join in.

Her eyes are filled with water about to leak,
And the world is blurred through her tears,
Her matted uncared for hair,
Flies in the wind,
Like branches swaying in the breeze.

The world has moved on and left her behind,
Leaving her swallowed in a hole,
And she's trapped - unable to escape,
And she's just aimlessly standing there,
Lost in her own make-believe world.

Fiona Webb (13)
Grenville College

Summer

Summer can sometimes be hot
But it can also be freezing
I use the whole pot of sun cream
And I use tissues because I'm sneezing.

Most of the day I'm on the beach
Or I'm having a game of football
I chill out by playing pool
Or by swimming in my lake

Kids boiling inside classrooms
While gardeners chill outside
Men in offices need a fan
While women outside get the sun.

Josh Taylor (13)
Grenville College

Me

You think I'm crazy,
Because of the way I live my life,
You think I'm insane,
Constantly living on the sharp side of the knife.

But you don't know me,
You don't know me at all,
I could be the Queen of Sheba,
Or the owner of the great China wall.

You think I'm strange,
So you tell your friends made up stories about me,
You think I'm deranged,
You want them to come after me.

Just because I'm different,
I tell you, that is all,
So you chase me home
And throw food at me in the school hall.

So many times I've had to move
To so many different schools,
Each time you come after me,
I'm different, I know, I don't try to be cool.

It can be unbearable,
I find that sometimes see
When there's nobody to turn to,
They're all against me.

I found life unbearable,
So it was the final straw,
When you said that you would get me,
Now I am here no more.

Imogen Strachan (14)
Hele's School

Normal

The little girl, just eight years old
She looked so much younger
Blonde hair, a sky-blue dress
It was keeping no secrets
The bruises could be seen by all
Her unnatural skinniness and pale complexion
It wasn't normal
The tough policeman, had tears in his eyes
The little girl's were wide with fear
They whisked her away, to a special place,
Where her mother couldn't hurt her anymore
She became strong, attended school
Suffered at the hands of bullies
But she fought back, persevered
Remained strong
Now she is sixteen, studying for her GCSE's
She is going to join the Royal Air Force
Nothing is going to stop her
She knows everything about her traumatic past
But she doesn't allow it to affect her
She's normal now.

Kate Rivers (16)
Hele's School

Destroyed Laughter

Laughter was a part of our world
Terrorism was not.

Terrorism is a part of our world now
Laughter is not.

Is it too late to turn back time?
Is it too late to undo the damage?

Abigail Ings (14)
Hele's School

The Journey

Panic,
A gunshot,
Piercing through my skin.

Heart rising,
Chest thumping,
But no point to beat.

Shedding fear,
Through the world,
No love in reach.

Eyes start to water,
Feeling heavy and mean,
Searching for an answer
Which can't be seen.

Confusion,
Spreading through my mind
Like butter.

Memories,
So dark and gloomy
Fill my head
And then and then
Nothing.

Laura Rice (12)
Hele's School

The Band

I know a band that doesn't sing,
It doesn't play,
It's not the king.
When I pull, it goes *ping!*
It's as stretchy as a spring.
Hey I think you're out of hand
Cos it is . . . *a rubber band!*

Amy Townsend (12)
Hele's School

Bravado - The Bull Fighter

A daring display of courage
Fulfilled to impress.
A brusque decision to go ahead
The fighter accepts the test.

Charging, the bull storms at him
Horns lowered, the bull is raged.
The atmosphere holding suspense
Other bulls wait - caged.

The fighter's cloak, like a wave of darkness
He slashes at the bull's flanks.
A gruesome entertainment, but victory clear.
The crowd cheer their thanks.

The bravado went on,
The next fighter in.
The next raging bull,
Still the fighter does win.

Then a change of luck as the last bull is released.
This one seems so different, more challenged by its foe.
His tail curls, whips and twists. His horse already bloodstained
He spins and bucks more fiercely, his sharp weapons low.

The fighter retreats.
This bull's too strong.
One way to escape,
But he takes too long.

And tearing his cape and demolishing his pride,
Then onto the victim, the bull drags him down.
The Spanish bull fighter is destroyed.
Now who's the clown?

Gemma Stewart (13)
Hele's School

The Terrible Ending

The deed was done
And he could not run.
Run for his life,
Or run to his wife.

He could see his fate,
He was the bait,
His head in his hands
It was the enemy's lands.

Looking at them all
Running like a bull
A bullet in the air
But like they care.

They're dirty and mean
And mighty unclean
I'm a wanted man
Public enemy number one.

I don't understand
Why I can sense evil in the land
I got my gun and ran round the bend
But then it was the terrible end.

Kurt Richards (13)
Hele's School

Dustbin Shadow

The shadow of the dustbin cat
Stealthy
Sharp
Quick and sly
Slinking in the unholy shadows of Dustbin Alley's eye
The rattle of the broken bottles
As the dustbin cat scrounges
In the blink of an eye
The cat has spun around
Striking out with lethal claws
Its eyes as cold as a wolf's howl
Are the eyes of the black alleycat
Its opponent
A ginger tom
Hissing
Spitting
Blood flows
And the ginger tom bows his head
To the king of the alley
And the shadow of the dustbin cat
Reclaims his territory.

Alexa Parker-Carn (11)
Hele's School

If I Won A Million Pounds

If I won a million pounds,
I wouldn't buy a pack of hounds.
I wouldn't buy a hundred cats,
Or a lifetime's supply of hats.

I might buy a huge white boat,
Or a castle with a moat.
Maybe I'd buy a fast, red car,
Or a trip to lands afar.

I could blow it all on clothes,
A girl can't have enough of those.
I could buy a house with acres of land,
Or a private beach of fine, white sand.

Maybe I'd buy a widescreen TV,
A video player and DVD
An Xbox and PlayStation for my own personal use,
Or pencils of every colour, including puce.

There are lots of things that money can buy,
A list that'd reach up to the sky.
But I wouldn't spend it all on me,
Buying lots of presents would make me just as happy!

Hannah Moran (12)
Hele's School

I Am An Animal

I have a soft fur coat,
I love to purr,
I rub my back on a post,
I have lots of fur.

I am so friendly,
I have sharp claws,
I play along happily,
I chase balls.

I am so kind,
I am so cuddly,
I have a clever mind,
I am very bubbly.

I crave food,
I chase mice,
I have moods,
I am nice.

I am a cat.

Hannah Hart (11)
Hele's School

Dartmoor

Dartmoor's treacherous landscape
stretches further and further,
crunchy underfoot
of what used to be the gleaming glory of the moor.

A grey, fearful prison stands threateningly
against the rugged backdrop in the distance
beside the contrasting warming pastels of
the glowing cottages.

Concealed mysteries lie hidden
within the undisturbed granite crags.

Matthew Bloomfield (11)
Hele's School

Dog

Dog:
A small, abandoned ball of fluff,
Owners had enough.

Dog:
Thrown upon the street one night, nobody to care,
Nobody to know that the dog was even there.

Dog:
Waits there on the street each night, loyalty to keep,
Waiting for his owner's voice, soft and deep.

Dog:
Still waits there on the street each night,
Now, tell me people, is this right?

Rebekah Cunningham (12)
Hele's School

My Cat Bracken

Purring softly in my ear,
As quiet as a deer,
She sits by the fire,
To make herself drier,
I get a cuddle,
After she's been in a puddle,
That way I'm . . . wet,
But she's my pet,
She puts her head on the bed,
After she is fed,
Then it's time to go to sleep,
Even without a peep.

Charlotte Bromley (11)
Hele's School

Sunset

Everything has its place in time,
the sun must fall behind the hill line.
Night-time will come around
and when it does there will be no sound
but till the moon shines, this summer day
hold your loved one close
and watch the sunset in the bay.

Ride your horse to the hills
and find shelter from the cruel world in the mill
but don't forget the time and place
where the sun will set its face.
The clouds are the glass
that guards the past,
so don't trouble this fair evening
release your mind and your heart.

Somehow the world is alight
with love and warmth
despite the wars across the shores
but everyone deserves a time
to watch the sun shine.
So enjoy the sunset and indulge in its beauty
for tomorrow it could be gone.

Holly Meaden (11)
Ilfracombe College

The Catch

Her day had come, but to us our night
As she stretched her wings preparing for flight,
Her sparkling jet-black eyes darted around
Watching for movement upon the ground.
Suddenly signs of life came from the east
Tonight there was to be a great feast,
For in the river that separated our land from theirs,
Swam a group of fish, undisturbed with no cares
Gracefully she spread out her wings, and she dived into the dark,
While she took a deep breath and screeched out her mark.
Crash landing down, her sharp talons spread out
She collected her prize - tonight it was trout,
Contented, she flew off home
To eat her supper all alone!

Georgina Hill (11)
Ilfracombe College

The Beach

The golden sand is so soft and warm
As it shimmers in the sunlight,
I walk beside the sparkling sea
The yellow sun is so hot and bright,
The fluffy clouds above my head
Look like cotton wool floating by,
The pale sky is so clear and blue
As the delicate butterflies fly.

Vicky Ratcliff (14)
Ilfracombe College

Poem

Hello words,
Nice to see you again
Order yourselves please
To make a clever poem,
Jump into my brain
Travel down my arm,
Then through my hand to the paper.

Please don't stop, words,
You are all important
Come to me and be written down
So you can be acknowledged
Please come to my head
There's a party going on
So come on, join in and don't be shy

When you are read you come alive,
So there's no point in trying to skive,
Come and join the celebrations.
All words are needed,
Even the tiny ones,
Words you are useful
So come and be magic.

Goodbye now words
Thank you for coming,
Please visit me again,
You are the inspiration for men
Thanks for the poem by the way,
It's been a blast
Whenever I need you
Please come to me fast.

Amy Batstone (13)
Ilfracombe College

Gone To Pollution?

Forever a shadow cast over the world
Earth's warming up, ice melting and curled
Darker than black and colder than ice
Shall this all make you think twice
Endangered species, littered floor
Coughing children, and dirty shores.

The earth is filled with human waste
Behind closed doors it's not all pretty and laced
There's nasty people and nasty things
No one's an angel with halo or wings
If you want the world to be around
In one thousand years, no birds, no sound.

It might have changed, no longer alive,
The last living creatures finding it hard to survive.

Rickie Adcock (12)
Ilfracombe College

The News

I'm terrified of terrorists
then George Bush came along.
He said he'd clear it up that day
but then it all went wrong.

George Bush is good? George Bush is bad?
No one can quite decide it.
Some people shout out war is good
and others try to hide it.

Now here we are in World War III
or so it sometimes seems
with big loud politicians
and terrorist regimes.

James Neubert (11)
King Edward VI Community College

The Eyes Of A Madman

Terrorist attacks all over the world,
Ruining the lives of others,
But some would say they are freedom fighters,
And think of them as brothers.

'You're looking through the eyes
Of a madman!'
Is what the adults will say,
When you mention the question of questions;
'Why can't we all be the same?'

Hunger and illness throughout the world,
Is nearly always ignored,
When some are really filthy rich,
Others simply can't afford.

'You're looking through the eyes
Of a madman!'
Is what the adults will say,
When you mention the question of questions;
'Why can't we all be the same?'

Injustice, it seems is all around,
And it's down to the human race.
We've started the problem and yet,
It's something we won't face.

So when I look through the eyes
Of a madman
There's nothing that I can't see
But when *you* look through
The eyes of a madman
You're actually looking through me.

Charlotte Fisher (13)
King Edward VI Community College

Failing And Falling

All will fail, all will fall, but not me.
Forever I will stay here, now I will not leave you.
Lying in your blood, falling, failing
And I will see the end of time with you, for I love you.
In all the grief that plagues our world
I will stay by you, for I will never fail, never fall.
My destiny lying here in autumn leaves
I will leave it all behind, the spring, the summer.
Sunlight on your face I can remember.
I have seen blood. I have seen spirits leave.
I have seen innocents slain.
I have seen lovers die in the blossom of their youth and life.
I have seen life, the ultimate giver.
I have seen death, the ultimate taker.
All I have not seen is apocalypse.
All I have not seen is peace.
In all the long years of the world
Still no peace.
As I lie next to you, your blood on the leaves
I wish for the end,
So that I may fail.
So that I may fall.

Poppy Struben (12)
King Edward VI Community College

No-Man's-Land

Utterly colourless concrete confinement
From the safety of the four walls
To the no-man's-land corridor.
The difference is evident.
What's your favourite name?
What's your favourite colour?
Who's your favourite god?
The watchers watch the torture
The scarring of the mind
The unanswered anguish in his/her eyes.
Stay out of their way, don't rise to the occasion, try to blend in
What extremes can a blender-in go to?
Out of the mouths of babes excretes the rankest poison
They stab the hardest
Deeper, deeper
And twist the knife - one, two, s**t in my shoe
Sweet -
Aren't they?

Betsy Porritt (16)
King Edward VI Community College

The Four Visitors

Each year, four visitors pass through my town,
first comes a young girl, wearing a bright green gown.
She weaves flowers in her long blonde hair,
sometimes she's happy, but sometimes she'll scare.

Each year, four visitors pass through my town,
second comes a young lady, wearing a bold orange gown.
She has rose petals in her long brown hair,
she is full of happiness and full of care.

Each year, four visitors pass through my town,
third comes a middle-aged lady, wearing a bright red gown.
Leaves tumble from her long red hair,
she is happy but she can roar like a bear.

Each year, four visitors pass through my town,
last comes an old lady, wearing a long black gown.
Icicles cling to her snow-white hair,
she waits in her kingdom left dying there.

Harriet Dodd (12)
King Edward VI Community College

You're As Useless As . . .

A film without a theme
A football without a team
A chair without any legs
A washing line without any pegs
A clock without hands
A country without any land
A sun without the shine
A teacher who's not on time
A shoe without a lace
A traveller without a case.

Amy Williams (12)
Lipson Community College

You're As Useless . . .

You're as useless . . .
As a lamp with no shade
As a worker not getting paid
As a bank with no money
As a bee with no honey.
You're as useless . . .
As a TV with no channels
As a door with no panels
As a bath with no plug
As a floor with no rug.
You're as useless . . .
As a table with no chairs
As a fruit bowl with no pears
As a match with no ref
As a person with no breath.
You're as useless . . .
As a city with no town
As a king with no crown
As feet with no heels
As a car with no wheels.
You're as useless . . .
As a bike with no pedals
As Britain coming home with no medals
As fire with no flames
As pupils with names.
You're as useless . . .
As Van Nistelrooy with no feet
As a budgie with no tweet
As a net with no goal
As a green with no hole.

Ryan McCarthy (12)
Lipson Community College

My Mum

They had quite a lot of classes, 30 people in each
They had house competitions as well
They had green, yellow, red and blue
They also had names like Mark, Matthew, Luke and John.

They had inter-house championships
They always won but sometimes they got the cane
That made them scream in pain
Outside they played a lot of games
Like hopscotch, skipping and even tig.

My mum's mum was pretty strict
She had to be in, dead on six
They went on picnics in the holidays in Milnrow Park
And ate some cool things like Spam butties
Morning coffee biscuits and drank a drink called spoo

When she went home to watch TV
It was black and white not colour like me
She said she preferred the colour TV
Not the three channels that you can't really see,
Her favourite programme was Bonanza
On the three channels that you couldn't really see.

Paul Decourcey (13)
Lipson Community College

Party Poem

Put the kettle on, Gretal
Lay the table, Mabel
Pass the cake, Jake
Don't be silly, Billy
I like your dress, Bess
Pass the popcorn, Dawn
Play a game, Jane
This is wobbly jelly, Nelly
Pass the pretty dolly, Molly.

Alexander Williams (12)
Lipson Community College

Summer Poem

Summer danced
Into the sand
Warming everything it sees
It burns, yes it does
Including birds, trees and bees.

Summer skipped
Into their lunch
Tasty, tasty
Then it's gone
Crunch, crunch, crunch.

Summer slipped
Into my body
Bringing a warm haze of feeling
Summer is no time to be dealing
Look at the sky's blue ceiling

Summer fell
Onto the floor
Winter is taking its place
Hide, hide or be frosted
When winter shows its face.

Ben Gomersall (12)
Lipson Community College

Koi Carp

Koi carp are very tame
You can always give them a name.
Koi carp are very colourful
And also very joyful.
Koi carp grow to very big sizes
You can feed them all devices.

Reece Chamberlain (12)
Lipson Community College

Angels And Devils

Good and evil
Good guys always win
Bad guys always in the bin.

Light and dark
Kind and devious.

Gentle and rough
White and red.

Sweet and sour.

I'm like an angel
And I'm also like a devil.

In school I'm sweet like an angel
And at home I'm nasty like a devil.

Girls are angels
Boys are devils.

Angels are kind
Devils are like pines.

Soft and rough.

That's what angels
And devils are like.

Leah Doidge (12)
Lipson Community College

Birth

Birth is like getting a watermelon out of a lemon.
Birth is like getting a brick out of cement.
Birth is like getting a tree out of a twig.
Birth is like getting a plant out of a leaf.
Birth is like getting a sun out of its shine.

Jodine Bunker (12)
Lipson Community College

Partytime

Lay the table, Mabel
Press the cake, Jake
Don't be silly, Billy
I like your dress, Bess
Let's play dollies, Molly
Get disco, Jo
Let's make a den, Ben
Let's go to the park, Mark
The lights are dim, Tim
Let's have some candy, Andy
Let's have jelly, Nelly.

Mark Davis (13)
Lipson Community College

Computer

I'm the cleverest friend you've got
I know everything
Switch me on and my face lights up
I get pushed down and moved around by my mouse.
My keypad gets typed so fast I run out of breath
I search the world for anything you want
You can ask me a question, I'll answer it in 2 seconds
I'll stay awake for as long as you want me to
How carefully you drive me, I still might crash
I might have a virus, but I don't need medicine.

Leah Webb (12)
Lipson Community College

Advice Poem Mother To Daughter

Don't wear make-up,
For it makes you look old
Be natural, be beautiful,
Stay as you are.

It's a big world out there
And I don't want you to get hurt,
Please, please,
Stay as you are.

You're at that age now
And you are what boys want,
Perfect and beautiful, go careful,
Stay as you are.

Maybe we could compromise
And I could let some things be,
Don't think I'm being easy,
It's just plain old me.

Nicola James (12)
Lipson Community College

Cat Kenning

Fur ball choker,
People lover,
Paw licker,
Tail sweeper,
Food lover,
Hairy stalker
Attention seeker,
Aloof walker,
Superior looker.

Jannine Penny (13)
Lipson Community College

The Summertime

I lay down on the soft sand
Looking into the bright sky
The waves roar against the rocks
As I look at the ball of fire
The people on the beach
Speak like a 24hr radio
The waves gather mates
As they grow stronger each time
The sun starts to glare down
Every step becomes a nasty burn
The cliffs stand still
As if they started to watch me
It's time to go
I climb to my feet
Having no cares in the world
Just the memories of this time
Spent in my favourite place.

Ben Higgins (12)
Lipson Community College

The Worst Day Ever

Today was the day I went back to school
And started acting like a fool.
I got told off by the worst teacher ever,
He said stop playing around and being clever.

Today was great but attitude was poor,
What can be worse than getting a C4.
A letter went home, now I'm scared,
The thoughts are hatching with things I can't bare.

I must try to regain my form of trust,
I know in my heart that it's a must.

Emma Johnson (13)
Lipson Community College

Nowadays

When we were your age
We never gave any lip
We watched westerns whether they were boring or not
We never had the internet or PlayStations
You lot nowadays are spoilt.

When we were your age
We hardly ever had sweets
We sat still and did as we were told
You relate us to loners
Who sat and read books.

You lot nowadays
Get spotlight
They never *shut up!*
We had meals
You lot have takeaways.

In our days
The streets were safe
We could roam free
You lot moan about what you
Haven't got,
Rather than what you have.

Sophia Lidstone (13)
Lipson Community College

You're As Useless As . . .

You're as useless as lightning without a storm.
You're as useless as a prescription with no form.
You're as useless as some colours that you really hate.
As useless as a fisherman with no bait.
You're as useless as a school with no books.
You're as useless as a model with no looks.
How bad are you, you stupid old thing!

Joanne Hookins (12)
Lipson Community College

Forever Sleeping

It all seems so real,
even though I'm asleep,
fluffy pink clouds and floating sheep.
Mountains up high
and edible leaves,
I try not to awake,
though I can't resist,
but it all seems so great,
don't want to leave.
Chocolate pavements,
under your feet,
but they grow back, wow, yippee
and I know I must,
but what if I don't?
What will change?
Oh well,
back to my life,
boring and plain!

Shadene Lewis (13)
Lipson Community College

Run Rabbit

Jumping high to the sky,
But don't know how to fly,
Fox runner,
Fence jumper,
Grass eater,
Hole digger,
Light skipper,

Carrot snatcher,
As I take a shot at the bullet dodger.

Jason Haswell (13)
Lipson Community College

Memories Of A Childhood Past

Casting my mind back, to so many years ago,
My memories, never seem to slow,
So many bad times, so many good,
Should I tell you, well maybe I should.

So, I was born, in a bed,
Feet came first and then my head,
Upside down, since the beginning,
Back-to-front, yet, still singing.
When I was a lot younger than you,
I had to be tough, what else could I do?

At school I was beaten each and every day,
I'd say one thing and tempers would fray,
I was made out to be a fool,
That's why I hated every second of school.
When I was exactly the same age as you,
I had to be tough, what else could I do?

Early mornings, I woke up at dawn,
I looked at every brand-new morn,
I'd work the land, with my family,
We had to work or there'd be no tea.
When I was exactly the same age as you,
I had to be tough, what else could I do?

Then I grew up, and left home at sixteen,
Ready for the world as a hard-working teen,
I found a noble job, caring for the ill,
I was their friend, not just some nurse with a pill.
When I was just older than you,
I had to be tough, what else could I do?

So now we're here, watching your life unfold,
I hope it's beautiful, like my mornings of old.

And now this story is over and done,
Go off; go well, yours has just begun.

Declan Kehoe (13)
Lipson Community College

My Town, Plymouth

My town, Plymouth, is really great,
The seaside town you could not hate.
The sky is nearly always blue,
Its honesty will astonish you.

Plymouth is a peaceful place,
Moving along at a steady pace.
It hardly ever speeds ahead,
Just carries on or so it's said.

The waves crashing on the shore,
You can hear them growl and roar.
The sandy beach with a few stones
And lots of people eating ice cream cones.

Over the cliffs a beautiful view,
Lots to see for me and you.
Where there's a bright, shining sun,
We shall have lots of fun.

Plymouth has something for all,
Leisure centre, beach and swimming pool.
There's a river, museum and a library too,
How much more is there to do?

There's a town with lots of shops
And a high street I think is tops.
An eighteen hole golf course,
Or you can go riding on a horse.

Now I think we're nearly done,
Can we fit it in, in one?
The sun setting over the sea,
Isn't Plymouth a great place to be.

Lana Vaughan (12)
Lipson Community College

Today

Today is bright and sunny.
Today flowers bloom in the green fields.
Today birds fly up high in the blue sky.
Today the sand sparkles by the ocean.
Today swimming pools get brighter than ever before.
Today you take off on a flight.
Today children enjoy it in the bright orange sun.
Today shops open up with excitement.
Today the whole day fills up with joy and happiness.
People swim today at expensive places.
Today posters are hung up easily as they are happy inside.
Today be happy with yourself, the corn moon fades away into a cloud.
Today I walked down some crinkled steps, it was like an Egyptian tale.
Today I dropped my library book
I picked up the book and imagined I was one, going on adventures,
Standing still.
Today I watched a fluffy, white cloud floating in the air
I wished I was on that fluffy cloud, floating.
Today I felt like painting in my mind, a picture.
Today Plymouth is a happy city. I wish it was like this every day.
Today the grass is greener than ever, children relax on it.
Today boys play football on the brand new pitch.
Today has been beautiful and I feel 100 metres tall.

Dayne Paull (12)
Lipson Community College

Tornado

I am like a coil constantly turning
I pick things up and throw
them around like confetti.
Sometimes I have a playmate
and we chase each other
On the outside
I am *angry*
but on the inside
I am quite calm
When I run
out of energy
I rest.

Georgina Gue (12)
Lipson Community College

Summer

Summer skipped onto the beach bay
Warming up and becoming a stray.

Summer danced all over the street
And had to be careful of people and their feet.

She went into a summer shop
And she thought she'd buy a bottle of pop.

She danced around the street all day
When she was gone the day turned to *grey!*

Tia Britton (12)
Lipson Community College

Love

Love is like a chocolate bar melting by the sun
Romance and flowers for everyone
The gentleness and passion springs in the air
And leaves everyone totally in love!

Abigail Gallagher (12)
Lipson Community College

Keep Out

As I walked through the park
I was alone and it was dark
I thought I heard someone call my name
It was me going insane
As I carried on walking
I could hear someone talking
I saw some children with a metal bar
They were smashing up a car
As I carried on walking
I thought there was a man stalking
But he was only dog walking
I was glad to get home and go to bed
I woke up in the morning
To find the day dawning
To look forward to the day.

Rebecca Smith (12)
Lipson Community College

Football Crazy

Rushing around getting their kit
Getting nervous only a little bit
They come out to the pitch
And line up in a ditch.

Jogging around into their position
This is great in 3rd Division.
The referee gives his whistle a big blast
And the ball has gone so fast.

Running around up and down,
The referee gives his frown.

Jamie Hall (13)
Lipson Community College

Disneyland

I went to Disneyland
I got a great new tan

I was walking down a street
I could not stand the heat

I went on all the rides
I was always on the slides

I was in a swimming pool
I thought it was so cool

But to top it off we were in a hurricane
But then I had to get onto a plane

I finally got home
I felt like I was alone.

Alexandra May (12)
Lipson Community College

Animals

The birds are singing in the tree
The cats are purring on the ground
The dogs are here to play
The guinea pigs are shouting, 'Hip, hip, hooray.'

The fish are swimming in the sea
The spiders are crawling on your knee
The tigers are scratching at the tree
The lion got stung by a bee.

The rabbits are jumping up and down
Just like me and you
Jump for five pounds.

Gavin Price-Horne (12)
Lipson Community College

Snow And Storm

Snow
It drops like a feather
It lies down like a person
It covers like a duvet
It's as white as a ghost
And its enemy is the sun
When it comes out
It melts him away.

Storm
The rain is a baby crying
The thunder is his hands and feet banging
The black clouds are his mood
The night is when he goes to bed
The sun is when he awakes.

Scott Robson (12)
Lipson Community College

Summer

Summer slipped
to the beach
making the waves sparkle
and the people warm.

Summer danced
and made everybody happy,
smiling at the children
as they splashed in the sea.

Summer fell
into the sea
and was swimming in the sea
It was a nice day for summer.

Sumaya Muganzi (12)
Lipson Community College

Fire

They use me all the time.
They celebrate my birthday on 5 November.
I can cook but I don't clean up after myself.
Some people can't come near me
Because I make them sick
And now I'm in trouble.
When I get mad they have to get the fire brigade in
To control me.
I hate pollution and because of that
I am used for a safer fuel so when I smell gas
I explode in rage.
I hate it that I have no friends
But who needs friends
When I've got the best friend in the universe
My mum, the *sun*.

Jodi Smith (12)
Lipson Community College

Home

Home is a place where you can feel safe
Home is a place where you can be warm
Home is a place where you can stay
Home is a place where you can eat and drink
Home is a place where you can sleep
Home is a place that you need to keep safe
Home is a place where you put all your stuff
Home is a place where you can play safely
Home is a place where you can have a pet
Home is a place where you can be loved.

Patrick Sweeting (12)
Lipson Community College

My Family

I have a dear old mother
who likes to look out for others,
she loves working with kids
she is a real whiz!

My dad's name is Bob
he likes to do the odd job
around the house and on the car,
he walks our dog way too far.

They go for walks in the woods
my dog chases sticks and likes to do tricks,
he comes home dirty and wet,
there is a bath ready with bubbles all set.

My brother Lee
spends all his time at sea
he is a chef in the Royal Navy
he is well known for his lumpy gravy.

Chesney Wilkes (13)
Longcause Community Special School

Animal Farm

I have a fluffy cat,
Who sleeps on a colourful mat.

I like to go on walks with my dog,
I have to be careful, as he likes to jump in the bog.

I sometimes go and see a cow,
It likes to jump in the air and do a bow.

In the field, I've seen a big green frog,
He always jumps towards the stormy fog.

Sarah Brimacombe (14)
Longcause Community Special School

World Nature

I walked along the path and I saw a blackbird,
suddenly a high pitched noise was what I heard.

I had to look up in the trees,
looking back were some big, yellow bees.

It gave me a fright and made me jump,
Then I fell and had a bump.

I started to shiver,
as I ran through the river,
to get away from the crazy bees.

I ran to the hill to take a large pill.
to catch my breath and hide in the mill.

Alex Lang (13)
Longcause Community Special School

Animals

At the weekend I saw a pig,
It was pink and very big.

My friend has a black and white rat,
It sat next to a lovely ginger cat.

I've been to the zoo and saw a snake,
It did a special trick with a cake.

In my garden I saw a big green frog,
It jumped around on the grass and chased my dog.

I've been to a farm and I saw a white sheep,
I ran very fast and fell into a heap.

Patrick Baldry-Lee (13)
Longcause Community Special School

Hobbies

At the weekend we like to watch wrestling,
Especially when the English are winning!

Manchester United play football,
Cristiano Ronaldo has been seen to sometimes have a fall.

Houston Rockets have won the NBA Championship in basketball.
Charles Barkley has had the odd close call.

England played Fiji at rugby,
Jonny Wilkinson was heard to shout out, 'Hug me!'

Jonny is our new England captain,
We like him and we don't want his manager to sack him!

Oliver Smith (13)
Longcause Community Special School

Sailing Boat

I was going sailing in my little red boat,
then it started hailing
and I started to float.

I was bobbing about on the swirling sea
minding my own business.
when suddenly a big wave jumped up and hit me.

I caught my breath and looked around
and there I was up on the ground.

My poor little red boat was scattered upon a mound
I waited patiently until found.

Daniel Huxham (13)
Longcause Community Special School

Feelings

At school today I was very sorry,
I smashed a window and began to worry.

I thought I might get into trouble and was afraid,
It was a game of football that I played.

My gut reaction was to feel quite sick,
One of the other boys started playing with a stick.

I pushed the boy over so he looked at the sky,
I didn't mean to hurt him but he started to cry.

The whole experience made me quite sad,
I was well behaved as I didn't get mad.

Gary Beasley (14)
Longcause Community Special School

Sport

I had a friend who played basketball,
She was very big and very tall.

There was a girl who liked to go swimming,
She was very good and always liked winning.

Many of the girls in the school play netball,
Some seem to struggle as they are too small.

Some of the adults went to watch the boxing
But unlike me I prefer foxing.

Yesterday we played a game of football
But it started to rain so we came into the hall.

Zoe O'Connor (13)
Longcause Community Special School

Gone!

I stood, I heard, I watched,
I listened,
I did all of these things
but nothing came of it,
So I turned and strolled away,
Left myself standing, staring, listening
but hearing nothing.
Once again I hear the voice,
cold as ice, warm as fire.
I ran, legs burning,
fading, fading,
everything leaving me,
and then gone!

Demelza Champion (13)
Paignton Community College

Killer Whale - Kennings

K illing monster
I ncredible fighter
L ife ender
L imb chewer
E normous predator
R aging hunter

W ave rider
H ungry eater
A nimal killer
L ethal danger
E xtraordinary survivor.

Carl Harding (12)
Paignton Community College

The Love Of My Heart

To Beatrice,

Oh my Beatrice, I shed thee love over blossoming with a
graceful hand
Offering love and comfort like a dove glistening with ebony white.
I will cast upon thee with the light, of which we together, shall follow,
Amongst the times when there is only darkness as far as the eye
can see.

Think of me as a rose that blossomed from a lily encased among the
waters of sorrow,
Quivering in the moonlight, to thy glistening plains of paradise.
Nothing shall blossom thee as your light of quicksilver gold,
Glinting as a ripple, lapping the sands of time, and you and me
together shall reach to the hands of Heaven.
There we shall lie together.

Always . . .

Benedict

Tristan Illman (13)
Paignton Community College

My Cat Tara - Kennings

Paper chaser
Fussy eater
Veggie hater
Happy napper
Drink nicker
Bird stalker
Furry cuddler
Sofa ripper
Love bringer

Sita Zapata (12)
Paignton Community College

Disgruntled Goat

Disgruntled goat in a shed,
Disgruntled goat in his bed.
Disgruntled goat that I once knew,
Disgruntled goat that bit my shoe.

Melancholic hamster in his cage,
Melancholic hamster full of rage,
Melancholic hamster in his bed
Melancholic hamster now is dead.

Suicidal bunny jumped out of the tree,
Suicidal bunny broke his left knee.
Suicidal bunny in a hospital bed,
Suicidal bunny will soon be dead.

Angry ant crawled down a hole,
Angry ant scratched by a mole.
Angry ant found by a man
Angry ant fed to a lamb.

Lloyd Porter (12)
Paignton Community College

Football - Kennings

F oul
O ffside
O wn goal
T ackle
B ooking
A ttack
L inesman
L eague

Craig Hughes (12)
Paignton Community College

Home Pets

One dog to love
One dog to feed
One dog to walk
One dog to need

Parrots that squawk
Parrots that walk
Parrots that can't talk
And don't ask why

Cats that play
Cats that sleep
Cats that run
Cats that eat

Hamsters that grunt
Hamsters that sleep
Hamsters that eat
Hamsters that run

Goldfish that swim
Goldfish that dart
Goldfish that float
Goldfish that die

Tarantulas that scuffle
Tarantulas that hunt
Tarantulas that scare
Tarantulas that hurt.

Jo Parnell (13)
Paignton Community College

The Love Of My Life

The sun shines when he is here,
I hope that he will always be near.
I live in fear that he will leave,
Don't go or else I'll grieve.
He is the last thing I think about at night,
I hate it when he's out of my sight.
He bought me a pearl,
I'm his only girl.
He keeps telling me this,
As he leans in for a kiss.
He has a lovely smile,
I would walk a mile
Just to be with him.
Without him, my life is grim.
It's lasted for so long,
We even have a song
It's called, 'You're Still The One'!
Don't ever be gone.
I love him in the morning
As the day is dawning.
I love him in the afternoon,
As the day looms
To the evening and night-time through.
We're stuck together like glue.
He tells me he loves me,
We will always be -
Together, forever.

Lisa Williams (12)
Paignton Community College

Your Smile

Your smile was the sun,
Rising at dawn,
Brightening my world for all of time.

Your smile was my flower,
Bursting into life,
Bringing amazing colour over the darkest grey.

Your smile was a flame,
Ever burning brighter,
Dancing upon your beautiful face.

Your smile is one memory now,
That will slowly fade away.
Drift into eternal darkness,
Forever to stay that way.

Kelly Knight (12)
Paignton Community College

Cat - Kennings

Flap user
Food finder,
Wool unraveller
House breaker
Mouse catcher
Dog scratcher
Affection giver
Night stalker
Rodent killer
Prize winner
Love giver.

Melanie Jenkins (13)
Paignton Community College

My Music

My music is loud
My music makes me proud
My music helps me sleep
My brother's happy because I don't
Make a peep!

Linkin Park are rock 'n' roll
I'll see them next week at the Hollywood Bowl.
Linkin Park are really cool,
My favourite song is 'Break From You'!

This is the end of my music poem
You're going home knowing
What my favourite band is
You'll never know - so goodbye!

Elliot Simpson (12)
Paignton Community College

I Wish He Was Back

Every day scurrying around
I wish he was back
Little pitter-patters going up and down
I wish he was back
Never getting one bit boring
I wish he was back
Getting people up because he's gnawing
I wish he was back
Yet they manage to get in a little smile
Even whilst they're yawning
I wish he was back.

Mitch Duffin (12)
Paignton Community College

My Poem

I am a witch
My name is Emma,
Have you seen
My cat, called Trevor?
I must find him soon
Or my spells won't work.
And then I will look
A silly old berk!
I can turn you into
A rabbit or a frog,
But not one that
A princess would snog.
The time is nigh
When I must fly,
So onto my broom
And into the sky.

Emma Gallacher (13)
Paignton Community College

My Little Fishy

He lived in a tank so he didn't need a bank.
We really miss him, I used to kiss him
through his tank.

I think about him all the time,
and remembered when he used to swim
I used to watch his little fin.

Oh how I miss him, but will never forget him.
I will always love him 'cause
he was my little fishy!

Lauren White (12)
Paignton Community College

Rameses The Second

Oh hear me people, I Rameses the second, command that
You will always remember, even though I ruled with fear.
You are important to me, I love you all dear,
I command that all of you should visit my temple
But when I'm gone, it will be up for rental.

I sincerely hope that I will be remembered by
My one hundred and sixty-nine children and my beautiful wives,
And hopefully I'll be remembered in all of your lives.
I will be remembered by my enemies with hate,
I hope you will spread their blood and use it as paint.

So my name will ring through time
As I ruled for 66 years, you must agree,
I really am the best there could ever be.
I hope you will remember me as a wonderful thing.
And I hope my catapults will make an extra loud *ping!*

Thomas Parker (12)
Paignton Community College

Murder - Kennings

Bone collector
Skull cracker
Eye gauger
Brain eater
Tongue nicker
Neck slitter
Bone breaker
Blood drinker
Teeth taker
Brain sucker.

Nathan German (13)
Paignton Community College

Teachers

My teacher is over there
Please no one, don't be scared
She just wants you to be aware

My teacher is over there
Look everyone, she's coming over here
She's even more near
So why do you fear?

My teacher is over there
She says she always gets home late
But I think that is just fate

My teacher is over there
She likes to laugh
But not like the rest of the staff.

Natasha Perry (12)
Paignton Community College

Rameses II

'Oh hear me my people, I Rameses
the second, command that
you will worship me and what I do.
If you obey everything, then I will too.

I will be remembered by my kingdom
that I loved quite dearly
and enemies that I didn't, quite clearly.

So my name will ring throughout time
because I reigned for many years and
did every last bit, in fear.

History I know, I will make,
I can, I will - no mistake.

Holly Hill (12)
Paignton Community College

Teacher

Teacher, teacher, how can you be so loud?
It makes me dizzy and you look really proud.
You are so mean, some think you're the Devil from Hell
Instead of screaming, use a whistle or even a bell.

It makes me sick to hear you set homework.
We are tired after school
So leave us alone or we'll turn nasty
And we'll cast a spell, to make your face look like a pasty.

Teacher, teacher, how can you be so mean?
Just because I'm late, you send me out
After five minutes or so, you come to me
You give me the evils, then you start to shout.

Can't you see who the hell you are
Just go from here, go really far
No one likes you, no one cares
We might as well just feed you to the hungry bears.

Vicki Wilding (12)
Paignton Community College

I Used To Love It When . . .

I used to love it when she talked, because
her voice was so gentle.

I used to love it when she smiled, because
her face always lit up.

I used to love it when I went round her house,
because she always gave me my favourite cup.

I used to love it when her golden yellow hair
shone in the sun.

I used to love it when she put on
her shiny lipstick

Katie Callam (12)
Paignton Community College

I Am . . .
(Inspired by 'I Am' by Liz Webster)

I am generous, loving and giving
I care very much about my family and friends,
My home is important to me
My accessories are important to me
The whole world is important to me.

Having a family is a good thing
But bullies are a bad thing.

The world is getting bigger.

The shorter the days, the more
beautiful they are.

People are too kind.
I am.

Leanne Hardwell (11)
Paignton Community College

A Poetry Poem

Words spilling around in my head
But won't come out.
Can't get out.

Is that a good word?
Is that a bad word?
Should it rhyme?
Shouldn't it rhyme?

Metaphors and syllables
Simile and stanzas
That's the way, that's how I am
Writing poetry? I can!

Isla Fawcett (12)
Paignton Community College

Frustrating Writing Poems

Words spinning around, whirling around,
I look for them, they can't be found.
Get out of my head, onto the page,
Now I'm really full of rage.

Rhyme seems to escape me,
Punctuation hates me.
Like doing an exam on a hot summer's day,
Begging let us out, let us play!

Metaphors and similes,
I will try with some help please,
Why will nothing go my way?
I should be finished by the end of the day.

That's a rap
              The end of the show
That's a poem ready to
                      Go!

Sophie Greedus (12)
Paignton Community College

Cinquains

Kittens awake
Purring with joy
Always misbehaving
Running around with cottonwool
Asleep!

Dolphin, she's there!
Squeaking with friends,
Our attention she wants,
Diving in and out of water,
Then gone!

Katie O'Brien (12)
Paignton Community College

The Wind

The wind crashed its way through my house
Its fist knocking all my possessions
down to the floor
Its feet ripping up the carpet.

A crack down my mirror
Its roaring face running
up my stairs.
I was running up the stairs
after it, trying to tidy up
its clutter.

It just didn't give up,
My heart was beating faster
than normal.

The wind lets out a roar
knocking me over as it flies
out the window.

Marcus Ogborne (12)
Paignton Community College

What Is Poetry?

Poetry is rhyming
Always climbing
Words binding

Poetry is imagination
With alliteration
And variation

Poetry is proper *bo*
Yo, yo, yo
Now I'm off *hooooome!*

Jack Williams (12)
Paignton Community College

No Sympathy For War

Dying mates who have lost their honour and
were covered by lakes of blood and screams of horror.

They were not even six feet under yet, but were treated
like starving homeless, the rich would rather forget.

During cold days, their eyes were white and dreams of war
haunt them through black night.

No church, no ceremony or coffin made from gold
or their secrets about war will never be told.

Trying to find the missing, who will never be found,
trod on the survivors dragging feet along dusty ground.

Get away! Run! Still remembered in my head,
Bang! Smack! Come over here, someone is dead!
But when I got there, it was too late,
Bold young man soldier, met his fate.
Going home with blood and gore,
Bearing no sympathy to my attitude to *war!*

Dominique Carr (13)
Paignton Community College

Christmas

The Christmas trees sway fast,
The ice is like ivy climbing,
But I'm cosy inside.

James Washbrook (12)
Paignton Community College

My War Poem

Explosions, banging, gunshots all around,
the wounded lie on the floor
getting bandaged, round and round.
The military scramble into no-man's-land
and are dropping like flies.
Getting over the barbed wire,
the enemy fight hard, shooting from
their trenches and tanks are blasting.
Bombshells are creating a field of fire.
Four weeks into the battle, the men are
physically tired.
Sitting with their families all day,
that is their desire.

The war is over, many lost their lives.
Now they've gone to a better place
waiting at the Pearly Gates!

Sam Dennis (13)
Paignton Community College

The Wind

The wind punched like an angry man
While he snatched the drink
And was dashing in bedrooms
He pushed me, I ran towards the door.

I could hear his stomping feet above me
And the bellowing down the banister
His face appeared as a shadow
Asking for nothing, he helped himself
Pulling paintings,
Crashing cupboards.
He was gone . . . quiet peace but messy.

Alexandra Keen (12)
Paignton Community College

Silent Cry

I look around, no one's there,
I look to the floor and then I stare,
Blood and bodies are all around.
It looks to me as if no one's been found,
Hurt and pain seeps through the air
There's no one else but me to care.

The wind is howling
The trees are scowling,
The world is in silence
Because we're stunned from the violence.

My silent cry
From what I see from my eye
Will haunt me, until I die.

Lauren Simpson (14)
Paignton Community College

Gone

She wanders through the dark,
looking for an answer,
lost in dreams, far from bliss,
cold and all alone.
Many whispers she hears,
along the mystic path.
She is alone, not loved or cherished,
lonely in her thoughts.
She thinks of what life would be without her strength.
There she waits, confined in her mind
without her fondness,
loved.
She waits there in silence,
up above, until she is gone.

Katy Biggins (13)
Paignton Community College

My Rabbit, Sparkles

My little rabbit Sparkles, has bright eyes
and a twitching nose.
One night of freedom and then all
your life goes.
I hope you don't sit up there
thinking your life was a con.
If I had known, I would have told your
old friend John.
And if I had seen, I would have
put up a fight,
For whoever did this had
furious spite.
I hope to see you again one day,
I wish to bring you back.
I'm so very sorry for that great
tragic attack.
I don't know whether it was an
owl or a cat?
But you must always remember
that I loved you like that.

Jade Cooper (14)
Paignton Community College

War Girl

The girls who sleep alone at night,
The girls who want their men back.
The girls who have to do their jobs, right.
The girls who don't want to get the sack,
The girls who stamp the tickets on the bus,
The girls whose men are in a terrible rush.
As they cook and bake their buns,
The men who shoot bullets from their guns.

Joanne Butler (13)
Paignton Community College

Liberating Women

There was the girl at your beck and call,
There was the girl who helped out at the school,
These women would always do
Whatever you wanted them to -
But not anymore!

When the war began, men went out
The women would run out and shout,
'Goodbye!' to their men
But then the great jobs began!

During the excitement of jobs in the war,
The women always wanted to do more.
Working in the sun and rain,
Working towards their own gain -
Just to prove they could do it.

They worked in big, heavy vans,
They had jobs in the train station.
Didn't need any help, didn't need a man,
Doing jobs with nice communication.

Emily Brown (13)
Paignton Community College

The Beach

The beach is warm to play upon
To watch the waves crash
To wet your feet and paddle through
It's the fun thing to do.

Water's warm at the edge, you know,
When the water rushes through your toes,
You can build sandcastles up, one by one,
As I enjoy this, because it's so much fun.

Samantha Gardner (14)
Paignton Community College

World War One Poem

When I look back over the war
I fill up with excitement and
Wish I could go back.
And remember all the girls
Doing the jobs the man used to do.
I feel they do it better.

They are becoming
Strong, sensible and fit
They're showing how well
They're doing at the jobs
They don't usually do.
I feel they do it better.

I'm glad I'm here,
Not where the men are.
I do feel sorry for them
But the men are better
At the 'hands on' things.
I feel they do it better.

Even though the war is over
I still think about what we were doing
To help people live.
We do what we do.
I feel we do it better.

Hannah Wilson (13)
Paignton Community College

Transport Trio

What am I?

Leaving a trail behind and speeding in style,
Trampolines all around me
More holes than a cheese slice
No not mice, I don't attract mice
When I'm up there.
What am I?
Answer: A plane.

Haiku

Sailing through the seas
All around me so calm
I might be sleeping.
What am I?

Answer: Boat and sea.

Cinquain

Got on, read the paper,
Also nearly there.
Speeding and speeding
Through the hole,
Got off!
What am I?

Answer: A train

Ilan Adam Strul (11)
Paignton Community College

Shattered Minds

Bodies strewn everywhere, all around me
Only a pool of men left.
The gas surrounds us as well,
We jam our masks over our faces,
So Satan's hand of theft
Doesn't take our lives away.
I look down, down into the trench
Where men die, their bodies so gay.
A dead man so queerly laid on a bench.
I found a photo near my boot,
Of a man's family, crinkled up.
The squelch of mud under my foot,
The loud, lasting fire of a
Single machine gun.
The lasting loudness of pain.

Michael Bradfield-Payne (13)
Paignton Community College

The War

The man was lying, hopeless
He was as pale as a white cloud,
The bombs were flying everywhere
Like fireworks, going wrong.

Watching your friend lying there talking and
with a snap of my fingers he was gone.
The man was lying, begging for his life.

Many people were injured and bleeding
like red spray paint.
So many people lying there, speaking
and as soon as you lifted them
they were dead.

Jade Hodgkinson (13)
Paignton Community College

Rusty

Something happened which changed my life
My companion Rusty
Came across a demon with a knife.

He escaped off his lead one winter night,
I chased dear Rusty
But he disappeared beyond my sight.

I search street upon street
But a bloodstained path
Is all I meet.

I follow the red trail in the hope
To find my friend
A sorrowful limp heap I see
It was Rusty's end.

My eyes glazed with many a sad tear
Unable to think clearly
My emotions hijacked through loss and fear.

Rusty my companion, my love
His life brutally stolen
Now his soul lives safely above.

How can a thoughtless act of violence
Take away my best friend?
Rusty lives in Heaven, in silence.

Sady Boswell (14)
Paignton Community College

My Fish Book Poem

In my fish book I will look,
At the fish that eat, swim and suck.
This fish I see with flame-red fins,
And eyes as bright as little pins.
With bright red fins and a curious nose,
Around and around the tank it goes.
Catfish are cute with whiskers so long,
Tickling the tank as it goes along.
They are so cute and ever so sweet,
And to top it all, they love tropical heat.
Puffers are strange, they eat with their beak,
And when they puff up, they look like a geek.
Puffers are fat and sometimes brown,
Which sit on a throne with a golden crown.
Kuhlii are loaches, which are so cool,
Despite their appearance, they are the fool.
They chase each other around the tank
And then they rest and look really lank.
Now I close my fish book,
But I haven't really begun to look
At all the different kinds
Of fish that look divine.

Emma Louise Bilski (13)
Paignton Community College

Roses

Roses are red
They smell so sweet,
They make the garden light up
They show off their beauty
So the world can see
What beautiful flowers
They can be.

Amber Baird (11)
Paignton Community College

Make That Poem!

Make it from a rhyme,
or feelings from a crime.
Make it make a sigh,
or make it, make a cry.
Make it to offend,
or make it good to send.
Make someone sad,
or make that someone mad.
Make it to express
or one to love you less.
Make one love you more,
or make their love heart sore.
Make it get what you want,
or use a different font.
Make a poem for goodness sake,
just make, make, make!

Fiona Bell (12)
Paignton Community College

Grandad

I sat upon the rock
In the moon's shadow,
The moon was so plain,
Against the sparkling stars.

I felt a gentle hand upon my shoulder,
I turned around
And there I found
The cold breeze, getting colder.

I looked into the heavens,
Where my grandad was
And prayed to God to
Look after him, that's all I want.

Joanne Mills (12)
Paignton Community College

Mr Prime Minister

Stop killing fox
Stop killing rabbit,
All this hunting's
A bloody habit.

For murderers and rapists
Throw away the key,
That's what I would do
If it was left to me.

Stop being selfish
Stop being dumb,
Wake up Prime Minister
Stop sucking your thumb.

Stop all the lies
Start telling the truth,
Stop being pathetic
Stop being you!

Vaneese Cox (12)
Paignton Community College

The Monkey

Sid the monkey is so good
You'd like to stroke him if you could
His hair is fluffy and brown
But sometimes he acts like a clown
They feed him twice a day with fruit
When he eats, he is so cute
Sid has started to doze
But it doesn't matter -
The zoo has closed.

Chris Lawes (12)
Paignton Community College

Honey, My Chihuahua Dog

Honey, my Chihuahua dog,
She loves tinned food with biscuits.
She has to wear a yellow harness
Honey is a racist to darker skinned people!

Honey, my Chihuahua dog,
Barking at dark people on TV.
She watches anything on TV,
Her toys are ripped or half eaten!

Honey, my Chihuahua dog,
Her chewing habits get her into trouble,
Running in the garden all day,
Or having a little snooze.

Honey, my Chihuahua dog,
She still can't walk on her lead!
The world is a toilet to her . . .
If only she could flush it away!

Connor Mills (12)
Paignton Community College

Cats

No animal is as cute and sweet
As a pussy cat around your feet,
Wagging its tail ready for lunch, and also
His biscuits to crunch.

Mice he likes to eat but when he comes home,
He asks for treats.
He watches and stares
As I eat my pears.

I love cats!

Emily Powell (12)
Paignton Community College

With Deepest Sympathy

First he was born,
His mum went down ill.
Within two weeks she died,
His nan took him in.

First day of school,
The bullying began.
That very same day his nan died,
Now he had no one.
He was all alone,
Apart from a few other orphans,
Who had been disowned.

First day of secondary school,
The bullying never stopped,
Then he turned to a life of crime
Shoplifting at any chance.
He then wanted to go to college
But he was turned down.

First day of being alone,
He went to his house.
The police were called in,
He was found hanging.
He had hung himself.
This is for him . . .
With deepest sympathy.

Matthew Jerwood (12)
Paignton Community College

My Year

Hedgehogs awake from hibernation,
Lovely plants come out to greet us
When summer flies to us, the sun blazes on us,
Our backs become redder and redder.
As autumn comes, crisp leaves fall to the ground,
Ready for us to crunch.
Conkers drop for us to destroy,
As autumn ends, winter comes.
Fighting through the snow
Getting ready for Christmas!

Christmas:
Cherish the moment, it's not every day you get one,
Happiness for all the family,
Rejoicing at this festive time,
Ivy covered the mantelpiece.
Santa comes and goes.
The baby cries in the manger, wondering what's going on.
My presents are what I wanted,
Angels celebrate the moment,
Singing joyfully.

Winter:
Fighting through the snow,
Dodging snowballs as we go.
Jack Frost comes and goes,
Bitter winds,
Gelid winds,
Oh so cold!

Paul Buckley (12)
Paignton Community College

When I Cry

He is never here anymore
A gentle, kind person, always there
Always cared. A sweetheart to me.

He is never here anymore
The smile I no longer see,
It's no fun without him.

He is never here anymore
He had an eye for food
From cakes to roasts
They're just as nice to him.

He is never here anymore
I never got to say goodbye,
So this is for you Grandad.

Lydia Hardy (12)
Paignton Community College

It Will Never Be The Same

It will never be the same since Nan died
Shopping bags are shopping bags
Never bought, never will.

It will never be the same
Her shoes will not be stepped into, ever again
Lying lifeless, no more walks or runs.

It will never be the same
The flowers lying there in the shop
With the lovely floral smell.

It will never be the same
TV remote's lying there still
Never to be pressed, day to night.

Benjamin Gerrish (12)
Paignton Community College

My Friend Is . . .

My friend is a yellow girl,
She welcomes the world with her sunny smile.

My friend is a red girl,
She enters the room with her warm smile.
When I'm sad she makes my heart feel warm,
and treats me so kindly.

My friend is a blue girl,
She keeps her cool when someone
gets bullied.

My friend is a brown girl,
She eats that much chocolate
I don't know where it goes!

My friend is a baby pink girl,
She is never seen and is so shy.

My friend is the bestest friend I ever wanted.
Her heart so warming and full of gold.
I would never let my friend get hurt,
or let anything happen to her.

Danielle Goldthorpe
Paignton Community College

Animal Cruelty

Animals have feelings too,
Birds, horses and kangaroo.
Why do we lock them in cages?
Why do we hurt them to cure our rages?

Let them live, happy and free
Instead of taking them from the sea.
Animals have feelings too,
Birds, horses and kangaroo!

Jordan Victoria Jones (12)
Paignton Community College

Our Dad

We knew the pain you had to bear
But now you've been taken from our care.
As we stood and watched you sleep
Your loving face made us weep
As we watch you in our dreams at night
Just hoping you could hold us tight.
The great love you had given
Was like an angel sent from Heaven,
Dad we are so proud
And our dad you'll always be.
The love you gave was from your soul
For all the loving things you did.
Our dad you'll always be
A true companion and a friend indeed
Dad we will always love you and forever more
Love from your children you adore.

Laura Searson (13)
Paignton Community College

In Praise Of My Mum

Come, let us sing
My mum has a son
Come, let us dance
Alex is the name of her son
Come, let us pray
He has a dog
Come, let us play
Her son has a PlayStation
Come, let us sing
My mum has a wonderful family.

Stacey Brown (11)
Paignton Community College

Games

Games are great,
Games are the best,
Video games will beat the rest.
PlayStations, Game Cubes,
Game Boys and SPs too.
First they were bad,
But then they grew and grew.

I love video games, they're cool and fun,
Just like Game Boys you take them on the run.
If their batteries turn out flat
Just recharge them,
See, it's all that.

Later on in life graphics will be great,
Unlike the past,
Now that's the graphics that we hate.

Jade Oaff (12)
Paignton Community College

I'm Running, Running, Running

I'm running, running, running,
I'm running for a race.
I'm running, running, running,
Everyone can see my face.

I'm running, running, running,
I've never been so fast.
I'm running, running, running,
I'm out of breath at last.

I'm very, very tired,
I think I did my best.
I'm very, very tired,
I really need a rest.

Lauren Cooper (12)
Paignton Community College

Cat's Characteristics

They can be as shy as a mouse
They can be as proud as a lion
They can be as friendly as a fly
But they have claws that sting like a bee
They can be as lazy as a sloth
Or as active as a puppy
But one thing is certain about a cat
No matter what
They're as chilled as ice.

Lloyd Franklin (12)
Paignton Community College

Epitaph For My Gran

She was not known among her friends for sadness,
She owned no wealth, nor did she want it.
Her looks would always make you smile,
She couldn't play an instrument or laugh all the time.
Nor would she try.
She didn't fight for glory, showed neither great need to
But she loved everyone
That was her one gift!

Tracey Landry (12)
Paignton Community College

Red Water

The crocodile moves slowly through the murky water,
Quietly waiting for its prey to come for a refreshing drink.
As the wildebeest drinks, the crocodile knows it's time to strike.
One deadly move and the crocodile claims its victim.

Shaun Ellis (12)
Paignton Community College

Terrible Trenches

The rain storms down,
Down into the trenches,
Mud is everywhere,
Bombs being dropped.

Wounded people left to die
As hungry rats crawl around,
Eating the wound without a care,
Bombs being dropped.

Blood flying in the air
Along with mud and pus,
Food lay rotting,
Bombs being dropped,
Bombs being dropped.

Maxine Halcro (13)
Paignton Community College

Stormy Sea

The sea is an angry monster
Beating itself up,
Ripping anything in its way
Violently crashing against rocks
Grabbing the walls of beaches.

The sea gobbles fishing boats,
Sweeping the tops of beaches.
Tearing the hearts out of sea creatures
Whirlpools swirling around like crazy,
White horses galloping fast.

Katie Moores
Paignton Community College

I Miss You Bruce

I miss you Bruce
It wasn't the same when you went,
I cried for ages,
Why did you go, nothing was wrong?

I miss you Bruce
No more calling your name when I want a cuddle,
People say you were just a cat, but not to me.

I miss you Bruce,
No one can replace you,
You were my best friend,
Now you're gone, I'll never forget you.

Emily Penwarden (12)
Paignton Community College

I Wish He Was Here, My Grandad

I wish he was here to smile again
I wish he was here to hug me again
I wish he was here to laugh again,
Or even play bingo again!

He was not in the chair,
Or watching TV in the corner
Never in the kitchen, doing the dishes
I miss him not being there.

It's all so quiet
Till Pepsi barks
Nan's upset and has a broken heart.
It's not the same since he's been gone.

Jemma Brown (12)
Paignton Community College

It's Boring Now

It's boring now
There's no finding him
No rustling in his cage.

It's boring now
There's no squeaking of his wheel
No whizzing around in his ball.

It's boring now
There's no holding him
No playing in his cage.

It's boring now
There's no watching him eat
No cleaning out his cage.

Charles Stanley-Bloom (12)
Paignton Community College

An Epitaph For A Gifted Woman

She was not known amongst her friend for sight,
She owned much wealth but threatened no might
Her looks would not deceive people despite the poor
She could not see the cause, no pain.
She didn't make fun or wonder why.
She wouldn't laugh out loud at people's misfortune
She never showed a tear and did not fear
She never liked it when they stared or even
When they laughed at her gear
She didn't fight in battle or hit and punch.
Showed neither great or wonderful
But still always made me feel special and safe.

Rose-Marie Timms (12)
Paignton Community College

My Dog

She always loved the heat
And sat in front of the fire,
But that doesn't happen anymore.

She always loved a fuss
And followed us everywhere,
But that doesn't happen anymore.

She always came in my room
And woke me up early in the morning,
But that doesn't happen anymore.

She always wanted to play
And ran around in the garden all day,
But that doesn't happen anymore.

I really miss her
And I will never forget her,
But I know she had a good life.

Ellis Platt-Lea (12)
Paignton Community College

Honour

Through the cover of darkness,
The silence of the night.
As the scared hearts of the young men,
Fight their way through enemy territory
With pride and honour.

Only the monstrous anger of the guns
Can drive these men to butcher each other,
Which can drive even the strongest of minds
To go insane.
They fight for freedom and nothing more.

Chris Baker (13)
Paignton Community College

Morning Of The Dead

The sun shone on the red field of blood,
Nothing moves,
The screams cannot be heard anymore,
Last night there was no mercy.

The fast rotting bodies fade,
They fade into the sunlight,
The sun burns the bodies,
Until something moves.
Slowly getting up,
Flying up into the sky
Like angels going up into Heaven.

Souls of the dead
Ascending to Heaven,
For a long rest of happiness,
Waiting for their families,
Waiting, waiting,
For someone they love.

Claire Smith (13)
Paignton Community College

No Honour

Through the silence of death
Comes fear for those to die,
What cries come of misery,
For those of husbands and fathers?
Sobbing from the last breath,
When others just stand and cry,
Over coffin to coffin.

What funeral is this for heroes,
Survivors, slouched just searching,
For what's left of freedom.

Stuart Dearson (13)
Paignton Community College

Football

Football is my favourite thing,
It's my favourite sport, I love to win.
I love to play and love to score,
My sister finds it a total bore.

I play for Kingskerswell, we're a very good team,
Playing professionally is my ultimate dream.
I play at left back and defend the goal,
Any game, any weather, wet or dry, hot or cold.

Thierry Henry is absolute class,
His skills, his shots, his pace is fast.
Zidane and Ronaldo make my top three,
You just have to watch them on tele to see.

Luke Steward (12)
Paignton Community College

Dylan's Prayer

You didn't ask if you could go,
My answer would have been *oh no!*
You couldn't ask the question why?
Your time has come to say goodbye,
I prayed you'd be allowed to stay,
But the angels came and took you away.
Your pains are past for that I'm glad,
Yet in my heart I feel so sad.
I know you are not far away,
Looking over me each day.
And I can't wait till we meet again
At those golden gates.

Rachel Mussett (12)
Paignton Community College

Ashes To Ashes
(In memory of Jim)

Spread my ashes where the north winds blow,
Spread them where the flowers grow,
Spread them high and spread them low,
Spread them near a place I know,
Spread them on the hilltops high,
Spread them in the moonlit sky,
Spread them wherever, just please don't cry.

Robert Michael Roskelley (12)
Paignton Community College

Hallowe'en

Hallowe'en, a bloodthirsty trinket
Full of black, deceit and death.
Nights get long,
The moon rises in the midnight sky.
Dead become the living,
Living become the dead.
Taste of blood in people's mouths,
Horrors become a fairy tale.

Charlotte Brown (13)
Paignton Community College

Hedgehog - Haiku

Stumbling across
Along the slippy surface
Prickles held up high.

Ethan Wilkins (11)
Paignton Community College

World Of War

As the day runs by
I run with it
Through blood and guts

Empty shells of used bullets
One after another hitting
Random targets

People crying, praying
That the trapped spirits be released
Into the realm of good

Some men calm themselves down
By sharpening sticks
They know where the trail leads
Into the fiery mouth of Hell.

Darell Andrews (13)
Paignton Community College

The Sea!

She's angry, her claws drag across the rocks like thunder hit,
She roars when the rain burns through her skin,
The sky had risen so she got higher,
She fell on the sand and dragged some away,
She eats the rocks with her big, long teeth,
Her eyes were bright, awake and blue,
Her hands clap together like two tigers catching their meal,
But finally the sun rises,
She calms
And lets the children play.

Lindsey Evans (13)
Paignton Community College

Impending Storm

Impending storm
Rain dropping everywhere
Like thorns digging into you
Impending storm.

Flashing lights finally come in the sky
The rain hits you with a thump
Dark and grim the streets would look
All because of the impending storm.

It's like in a film, a new beginning
The smell is different, as if it was spring
The streets were fresh.

Ami Hopkins (13)
Paignton Community College

The Haunted School

Ghosts all around
Disappearing teachers
Lockers flying, open and closed
Haunted!

Sophie Poole (11)
Paignton Community College

Autumn Days - Haiku

Falling flowers sway
Bonfires light up autumn nights
Smoking fireworks fly.

Simon Nicholls (11)
Paignton Community College

My Mum Is A Pink Person

My mum is a pink person,
She is a flower blossoming each day.
Sparkling as the morning dew,
Tight bud when she's asleep.
Injecting love when she's in full bloom,
A protecting angel flying on the breeze,
Turning pink to red then bronze,
When the sun goes down.

Jordan Colledge (13)
Paignton Community College

The Sea

The sea is a baby fast asleep in its cot,
Its toes touching the sand.

Suddenly a storm brews,
Waves crashing against the rocks,
Mountains of water destroying everything in their path.
The baby has woken up
But all is calm again
As the baby's mother sings it back to sleep.
The sea is a baby fast asleep in its cot.

Dale Steadman (12)
Paignton Community College

The Sea

The sea
Rushing or still
It is fun and deadly
It is home to many creatures
Killer.

Michael Hughes (11)
Paignton Community College

My First Love

He was my first and only love,
His hair was as white as a dove.
His lips were dark and blue,
His love for me was deep and true.

My love for him was exciting and new,
My feelings were lasting and true.
My hopes are that we will be together,
Forever and ever and ever.

Hannah Cooney (12)
Paignton Community College

Animal House

I have a tiger, a fluffy-faced tiger,
She works all day, home and away.
She's kind, loving and gentle,
She never lets a person down.
I call her Mum.

David Healy (11)
Paignton Community College

Christmas - Haiku

Twinkling lights shine
Star on top of Christmas tree
Snow is everywhere.

Bryony Young (11)
Paignton Community College

Boy War

Gruesome war, fires ablaze,
Smoke choking, soldiers brave.
Slaughtering death, bitter life,
Blinding eyes, guns a-fire,
Bodies rotting, but one survives.

A boy, alone, unsafe,
One boy left, powerless to all kind,
Choking, choking with a bit of life inside him,
And he says, 'Help! Help me please!'
But no one's there . . .
To protect and keep him out of danger,
He was boy at war.

Hannah Gladman (13)
Paignton Community College

Winter

Winter, winter, winter's here,
Time to laugh with fun and cheer.
With lots to do and lots to see,
Let's put up the Christmas tree.
There's decorations here and there
And a festive feeling everywhere.

There's ice and snow on the ground,
Not a piece of pavement to be found.
Children running with lots of snow
While the adults run with the mistletoe.

Cheer up, come on, it's only winter.

Harry Clay (14)
Paignton Community College

War

As the enemy charges
It kills like a bird of prey
They run with guns and cannons
The sound of shrieking guns shooting
The cannons firing
The blood-curdling screams
As they fall to the ground
I lie still in the muddy trench
I remember my wedding
So calm, so peaceful
How times have changed
Oh I miss my girl
Her sweet delicate face
Not a hair out of place
Now I look into the mirror
Who is this looking back at me?
This sad, pitiful man
Who's been torn, limb from limb
What have I done?

Emily Barnett (13)
Paignton Community College

Cats

I love cats,
I love their long, lip-licking tongues
I love their long lashing tails
I love the fact that they're
All so cute, sweet and innocent looking,
But mysterious and dangerous.

Catherine Hougardy (13)
Paignton Community College

My Dog Guinness

My dog Guinness looks like a beer!
Black on his belly and white on his ear.
He runs down the garden, chasing his tail,
When the postman's here, he eats up the mail.

I take him walking, so he can be seen,
When he gets back, his coat needs a clean.
He's all washed and ready to eat,
The bowl's always full of biscuits and meat.

My dog Guinness is as hard as an ox,
All my friends just think he rocks.
He needs a friend to keep him from fear,
And that is why I am here.

Adam Westwood (13)
Paignton Community College

My Dog - Kennings

Paper taker
Stick fetcher
Cat hater
House chewer
Ear scratcher
Cat hunter
Stick catcher
Bone burier
Tail wagger
Hug lover
Love giver
My Murphy . . .

Katie Rees (12)
Paignton Community College

Eminem - Kennings

Cap wearer
Tight trouser hater
Car trasher
Closet cleaner
Swear word master
Blonde dye lover
Rap maker
Legend rapper
Shady caller
Eminem trooper.

Ashley Millar (12)
Paignton Community College

Villa

Aston Villa was a young team
At them the fans used to scream
Villa wanted that cup and good luck
On the shelf it would sparkle and gleam.

Stephen Swann (12)
Paignton Community College

Yummy

It's yellow, foamy, sour and gummy,
In my mouth then to my tummy.
My sweet is so sparkly and yummy.

Bumpy, bendy, cheesy, curvy,
The pop makes my tongue go topsy turvy.
My crunchy Quaver is so lovely.

Sadie Robinson (13)
St James' High School, Exeter

How To Eat A Boiled Sweet

First unwrap
The heavenly treasure
Rattling in its
Crystal glass wrapper.
Loving every moment.

Observe the ruby
Coloured treasure
As if it were the crown jewels but
More to come.

Next close
Your lips around
The ruby prism
And endure the

Succulent taste
As if it were
Surfing on the
Tip of your tongue.

Suck the
Jewel, don't
Let it go, just
Keep sucking
While it dissolves
Like an Aerial
Washing tablet

Now slurp,
Suck, let it
Juice and
Invade your
Taste buds.

Until it's gone.

Now take another one!

Cogan Westlake
St James' High School, Exeter

How To Eat A Boiled Sweet

Stuck in an oval-like
Prison, screaming,
'Let me out!'
Look. Don't taste, don't smell,
Just look at the lemony thing.
Observe with the eye,
Yellow and sweet
Then rustle the wrapper
Like a mouse sneaking in the night.

Feel the feeling in your fingers,
Like a sticky moon, high
In the blackened sky.

Next, pop in your universe,
And let it orbit like a spaceship.
Feel the numbness,
Lemon sweet.
Plastic wrapper abandoned, no sound
Will come from that.

Now the sweet's gone,
No taste, no smells
Just a feeling of
Hard boiled loss!

Zara Broughton (12)
St James' High School, Exeter

Wacky Winter

I looked outside the window,
To see what I could find.
I saw a load of white stuff,
It's messing up my mind!

I went outside to check it out,
It's really quite a mess.
'Cause I went outside to check it out
In a red, late summer dress.

'It's rrrreeally, rrreeally frreezing!'
I shouted really loud.
I ran inside the house real quick,
But the cold followed like a cloud.

I ran out with a coat on,
To check it out again.
I'll try to stay out longer,
But I don't think I can.

I picked up the white stuff in my hand,
It turned to water instead.
I ran inside the house again,
I think I'll stay in bed.

Aydan Gasimova (12)
St James' High School, Exeter

How To Eat A Boiled Sweet

First, unwrap the colourful gift,
Crackling in its
Crystal-like wrapper.

Surfing on the tip of your tongue
Rolling it around
Your mouth-watering jaws.

Next, taste the juices and feel
The smooth edge.
Hear the sweet, banging against
Your teeth.

Touch the sweet
And feel it glide
Across your fizzing tongue.

Jamie Bassett (13)
St James' High School, Exeter

The Average Day

Winter is cold,
Winter is freezing,
It's flippin' annoying,
It keeps her sneezing.

She's shivering, it's cold,
The wind's blowin' hard,
She gets to the pub,
And remembers she's barred!

She stands at the bus stop,
Got a cold and cough,
Getting out her ticket,
Freezin' her toes off!

Gemma Toy (12)
St James' High School, Exeter

Sweet V Quaver

You are ugly. You are smelly,
You are a Quaver.
You are sugary. You are beautiful,
You are a sour sweet.
With your dummy shape and your sugar-coating,
You are a sour sweet.
With your horrible cheesy smell and
Your horrible cheesy taste,
You are a Quaver.
You smell like my feet.
You are a Quaver.
You are like my deodorant,
So fine and great to have.
You are a sour sweet.
In my eyes the sweet wins,
As the Quaver cries.

Ryan Beckett (13)
St James' High School, Exeter

Winter Poem

Snowflakes dance and float in the wind,
The snow, thick and deep, freezes your feet.
The solid ice, cold and slippery.
The wind howls, the trees rustle, wildly.
All the leaves have fallen off the trees
Onto the white blanket of snow.
Winter is coming to an end,
The sun comes out.
All the snow and ice has now melted into large puddles.

Chloe Meredith (12)
St James' High School, Exeter

Winter's Here

Snow falling
From the sky.

Winter's here
Oh my, oh my, oh my!

Leaves scattered on the ground
The trees start to die.

Winter's here
Oh my, oh my, oh my!

Christmas comes, Christmas goes
Stick your teeth into a warm mince pie.

Winter's here
Oh my, oh my, oh my!

Jade Ashelford (12)
St James' High School, Exeter

Winter Fun

As the winter breeze is blowing,
The embers on the fire are glowing.
We wait impatiently for snow,
And when it comes, it's off we go.
Chasing snowflakes with the wind in our hair,
We breathe in freezing cold fresh air.
And when our hands and feet are numb
We know that we have had our fun.
So back inside to get warmed up
We're handed hot cocoa in a cup.
It's off to bed to sleep all night,
We will wake and have a snowball fight.

Lauren Meredith (12)
St James' High School, Exeter

Nah!

Nah! I'm not gettin' up today,
Der is no way dat I am gettin' up today!
Ya can yell an' shout, and frow me out,
But I ain't gettin' up today!

I ain't gonna sleep tonight,
Nah! I ain't gonna sleep tonight!
Ya can moan and groan,
But I ain't gonna sleep tonight!

Nah! I ain't goin' ta school dis mornin'
Ya can't make me go ta school dis mornin'!
Ya can eff an' blind, cos I don't mind
Nah! I ain't goin ta school dis mornin'!

Jennie Hamer (12)
St Luke's High School, Exeter

No'ting Poems In The Style Of Me

There is no'ting that I can do,
I can do a lot, a lot more than you.
I can prance around, dance 'n' sing,
In fact I can do anyt'ing!
Dere are sum dimwits, idiots of kings,
And they don't do a single t'ing,
So I says to you, 'Be original
And do the best that you can do,
For at the end of the day,
There is only one way
And that's to do no'ting!'

Spike van der Vliet-Firth (12)
St Luke's High School, Exeter

The Winter Season

As the blazing fire burns,
The weather outside twists and churns.
The fields are covered in icy frost,
All the plants are bare and lost.
Trees stand still and old,
Crispy leaves turn to gold.
As wind howls around the house,
Animals hibernate, including the mouse.
The robin looks out from its nest,
Showing off its bright red chest.
No more barbecues in the evening,
Just cups of cocoa, hot and steaming.
Marshmallows being toasted,
Christmas cards being posted.
Advent calendar chocolates every day,
Soon Santa will be on his way.

Katie Snow (11)
St Wilfrid's School, Exeter

Smelly Boy Jim!

There was a smelly boy called Jim,
Who always liked to play in a bin.
He'd never had a bath,
But he always had a laugh,
That was the life of smelly boy Jim!

Philip Birrell (11)
St Wilfrid's School, Exeter

Christmas Eve

The Christmas tree is up,
The lights sparkling bright.
My advent calendar is empty,
Presents wrapped up tight,
I'll sleep all through the night,
While Santa flies around in his sleigh,
With Rudolph leading the way!
I'll wake up in the morning,
My dad will still be snoring!
My mum will cook the Christmas dinner,
In the games that we play, I hope I'm the winner!
The day is nearly over,
It's gone so very quick.
Christmas is here,
I can't wait until next year!

Chantal Payne (12)
St Wilfrid's School, Exeter

My Favourite Food Is Brussels Sprouts

My favourite food is Brussels sprouts,
My family dislike them with no doubt.
I pile them high on my plate to eat,
With sweetcorn, potatoes and lots of meat.
They're green and yummy with flaky leaves,
Get off my sprouts! Get your own please.
They're round and tasty for you to chew,
They're healthy vegetables with vitamins too.
I have to let people have their own say,
But I think sprouts will win any day.

Natasha Durman (11)
St Wilfrid's School, Exeter

Autumn Shades

Dark red, yellow, orange and green,
Lovely warm autumn colours are all around,
The forests are full of these wonderful shades,
Hundreds of leaves falling gently to the ground,
Children love to play in the rustling leaves.

Bright ochre, pink, purple and gold,
The setting flames of the sun,
The sky is full of these wonderful shades,
Now the autumn season has really begun,
The birds are gathering to migrate.

Aqua blue, turquoise and sparkly white,
Merging shades of the vast ocean,
The sea is full of these wonderful shades,
Tossing and turning with never-ending motion,
Families warmly wrapped for combing the beach.

The ever changing colours of autumn
Remind me about the wonderful world in which we live.

Jordan Wills (11)
St Wilfrid's School, Exeter

The Bane Of The Boozing Leprechaun

There was a leprechaun named Stooz,
He had an obsession with booze,
He boozed all day
And he boozed all night,
Resulting in a rather long snooze.

One day he noticed something wrong,
His nose had grown quite long,
He was unemployed
And easily annoyed
And was really starting to pong.

He played his banjo, though very tough,
And in the streets he'd busk for stuff,
Vodka, lager, cider and ale,
He'd drink and never have enough.

One day whilst having one of his kips,
In came the apocalypse.
But in his life he'd achieved something,
He'd won the beer-drinking championships.

Luke Oliver (11)
St Wilfrid's School, Exeter

The Perfect Christmas

Crackers go *snap!*
The turkey is cooking,
Mistletoe hangs,
The children are looking . . .

At their presents under the tree,
Snow outside,
As white as can be.

The fire's burning,
Crackle and *pop!*
Tinsel shines
And baubles . . .

Drop because the cat hits them.
Oh, what fun we had today,
I know it's one, whole year away,
But I just can't wait!

Ashton Snow (11)
St Wilfrid's School, Exeter

Red Memories

Long have the poppies grown,
On the blood-soaked Flanders fields,
Memories of fire we own,
Thoughts of anger as we ran, close on our heels,
In the trenches we nurtured our hatred,
Ready to climb when the whistles blew,
On no-man's-land, fire and bullets dominated,
Gun at the ready, there I heard a, 'Coo,'
And there it was, a blood-drenched dove,
Perched steadily on the barrel of my gun,
It was the sign of hope, the sign of love,
It flew up high, up to the hazy sun
And the silence came,
In 1918 at 11 o'clock, peace would reign.

Erik Jellyman (13)
South Dartmoor Community College

I Know A Place

Scarves of amber mist loom toward you
As the harmonies of dawn applaud you
The red sun rises; a beacon to reward you
For your troubles: All is still as still.

A lake of crystal, clear as glass
A mystery to those who pass
A curtain of water onto bittersweet grass
Pure and true: white noise.

Wise old oak, a dark, rich jade
On top of hilltop as noon begins to fade
In the heart of wood there stands a mighty glade
Of sinewy elm with untold poise

Apple trees laden thick with fruit
Sweet, yet bitter, grown from the root
Subtle chill of autumn sunlight; silent, mute.
Heat of day, starts a spark, so flaming leaves burn.

And when I have used up all my days,
Seen the sky a thousand ways
Travelled the world, watched zebras graze
Here I shall return.

And I shall sit beneath the trees of old
And bathe in the stream, crisp and cold
And watch the crimson meadow turn gold
Still this shall be my home.

Jaye Noble-John (13)
South Dartmoor Community College

My Beloved

Surprised by you, every day
Sunrise lets me learn more
About you. About me.
Fingertips the teacher.

Your heart, binding mine.
Filling in the gaps.
My wrong answers,
Your right questions.

You are pieces shaped to fit
Hand in mine.
In sunshine and mist
Storms and darkness.

Resting head on your shoulder
Sees your chest rise and fall.
Touch a cheek of a face
I know better than my own.

Through these moments
Never lost a butterfly,
With your every tender kiss
They explode to life.

Fern Rhys (18)
South Dartmoor Community College

Let There Be Silence

Holes, come swallow us down
From this crazed and horrid town
Where all is lust and nauseous frown
Let there be nothing.

Darkness let the street noise be silent
Ghosts all standing, poised, violent
Laughing at all torment
Let them feel their own blows fall.

Knives come, fall, stab and choke
All those lives that streets have broke
Laughing shadows inhaling smoke
Let them scream to death.

Bombs come blow us through
Squeeze all the rubbish backwards blew
Kick out the cruel towny crew
Get on your knees, beg for mercy.

Holes, come swallow us down
From this crazed and horrid town
Where all is lust and nauseous frown
Let there be silence.

Leonora Wood (13)
South Dartmoor Community College

I Lost My Smile Blues

Oh, woke up this morning, it was halfway through school.
Whoa, woke up this morning, it was halfway through school.
Alarm didn't go off again, I feel such a fool.

Mum moans, teachers moan, friends complain about why I was late.
Yeah, Mum moans, teachers moan, friends complain
About why I was late,
Yes I lost my smile at precisely ten thirty-eight.

But next, it doesn't get any better, it only gets worse.
Well, it doesn't get any better, it only gets worse.
At home I left my school book and my purse

Now I'm starving hungry and the corridors feel cold.
Hey, I'm starving hungry and the corridors feel cold.
Well at least I can say my smile's retired and grown old.

No! Maths is still to come and my brain's bouncing off the walls.
Maths is still to come and my brain's bouncing off the walls.
If only I had the strength to stand tall, please don't make me fall.

Yeah! Home time is here and I have been made to feel so small.
Home time is here and I have been made to feel so small
And at home on my bed, left my little dog waiting for me,
I think I left my smile at home after all.

Sophia Rose Oliver (13)
Teignmouth Community College

The Morning Blues

Well I woke up this morning, so snug in my bed,
Oh, I woke up this morning, so snug in my bed,
I didn't ever want to lift the covers from my head.

Well I looked in the mirror, my hair was a mess,
I said I looked in the mirror, my hair was a mess,
I couldn't even be bothered to get dressed.

Well I walked down the stairs, my breakfast fell on the floor,
Whoa, I walked down the stairs, my breakfast fell on the floor,
So I couldn't eat anything so I closed the door.

I was at school and I sat on my desk,
Yeah I was at school and I sat on my desk,
The teacher asked me a question so I just had to guess.

It was lunchtime and I fell on the floor,
Yes it was lunchtime and I fell on the floor,
My crush walked past and I felt like a fool.

After school, I went to my mate's,
Well after school, I went to my mate's,
We went down town to go crabbing but we forgot the bait.

Laura Holland (13)
Teignmouth Community College

My Late School Blues

I woke up on Thursday and I was so late.
Yeah, I woke up on Thursday and I was so late.
I looked at the time, damn, it's half-past eight.

I went in the shower and I put on my clothes.
Ooh I went in the shower and I put on my clothes.
I felt really tired, I just wanted to doze.

I said, 'Bye,' to my mum as I walked out the door.
I said, 'Bye,' to my mum as I walked out the door.
I knew I couldn't sleep until half-past four.

I walked into school and I walked down the hall.
Yeah, I walked into school and I walked down the hall.
I was so scared, I knew my teacher wouldn't think this was cool.

I tried hard to pay attention, I tried every way.
I tried hard to pay attention, yeah, I tried every way.
Then before I knew it, it was the end of the day.

Sarah Olding (13)
Teignmouth Community College

Night

When the sun sets on the horizon
And darkness descends upon the Earth,
You can see no hand in front of you
And can only hear silence.

The night is a burglar, fast as can be,
It steals sight and hearing, so touch is left,
It conceals thieves, cloaks killers
And casts its deadly shadow everywhere.

It casts fear into the heart of the living
And gives strength to the minions of Hell,
Its eyes see all and whispers make rocks crumble
And it's only a blanket of darkness.

Finally, after hours of this torture,
Light penetrates the darkness
And as the first bird sings in the distance,
Darkness fades away.

Scott Parnell (13)
Torquay Boys' Grammar School

Changing

One tonne of solid stone shining in the scorching sun.
Arrogantly parading his muscles,
Demonstrating his overwhelming strength.

Time passes.

Ivy creeps over the fading leader.
A thick layer of bird droppings
Covers the decaying mass of unrecognisable stranger.

Time passes.

An age of abuse and assault.
The featureless lump of deteriorating marble
Dissolves into the changing environment.

Time passes.

The ancient mass of unrecognisable marble
Drifting for 2000 years further away from civilisation.
It is forgotten.

Tom Porch (12)
Torquay Boys' Grammar School

Personification Poem

My alarm clock went mad today
At 7.11 he made me pay
For setting him to wake me then
It had replaced my ancient hen.

He yelled at me and said: 'Get up,'
But I refused and said: 'Shut up.'
He pinned me down upon the floor,
I wrestled back but hit the door.

I let him go, he jumped at once
I kicked myself for being a dunce
He stood up straight, prepared to pounce
But with my energy's every ounce,

I stood and grabbed my cricket bat
It smacked the clock and knocked him flat.
My alarm clock went mad today
At 7.15 I made *him* pay.

Roger Doxat-Pratt (12)
Torquay Boys' Grammar School

The Gardener

The gardener has green fingers,
He knows what there is to know,
About flowers and plant life,
And in his work it shows.

He goes around with shears,
Cutting down dead plants,
But always being careful,
Of honey bees or ants.

He uses all his tools,
In the proper gardeners' way,
He's happy with his job,
And he does it through the day.

His dream to tend all gardens,
Big or very small,
Mowing and cutting plants,
Spring, right through to fall.

Sam Grace (12)
Torquay Boys' Grammar School

Death

He comes around so quickly,
Leaving a deadly trail,
He stops the hearts of living,
No need for the Holy Grail.

He dresses in black cloth,
He creeps on his white feet,
He smells death with his crooked nose,
No longer you hear his victim's heartbeat.

His enemy is Mother Nature,
For he hates the thought of birth,
He would rather watch a body,
Being buried in the earth.

He grumbles, he stumbles,
He's an insult to man,
But he doesn't care, for he is Death,
Avoid him if you can.

Alex Hambis (12)
Torquay Boys' Grammar School

The Evil Dog

The little dog has skinny legs
That are the size of wooden pegs.
A long pair of boots, crumpled up
And a creature's legs standing up.
Wet is the road, damp and shiny
Reflecting an image of the dog that's tiny.
The creature is a horse with badly bruised feet
With very long toes that fail to meet
Lines going up, lines going down
On trees and legs all around town.
The dog's head tilts from side to side
His eyes are evil and extremely wide.
Trees in the distance, leaves on the ground
Easy to see that autumn's come round.
Walking slowly along the broad and grey road
With a dog, small enough to be mistaken for a toad.
Why did they stop? What have they seen?
The dog knows for sure
Even with a brain like a bean.

Josh Papanicola (13)
Torquay Boys' Grammar School

The Legend Of Atlantis

The sculpture standing tall and gleaming with gold,
Wise, handsome face reigning over the land.
Its proud posture powerfully held.
Time passes . . .
Gleaming sword and diamond eyes,
Now wrenched from their sockets.
Standing tall but not proud,
Arms dented. Rusty, eyeless face,
Almost contorted in an expression of pain.
Five hundred years pass like rolling stones,
Washing over his head.
His once powerful hand striving out.
Only fragments remain, eroded,
Millions of miles away.
Two thousand years on,
Totally submerged in the lost city of Atlantis.
Myths and legends surround,
Making him once again unimaginably powerful,
Standing proud over passing fish.

William Kember (13)
Torquay Boys' Grammar School

Tribe

My parents died during the war,
When I was but days into this life,
Me and my friends furthermore,
Bound to fight for our tribe.

And now as we walk into battle,
Martyrs of our people,
Walking on the fields on which my parents died,
No fear of the sequel.

We are soon to be impoverished,
Our furthest hopes astray
And tomorrow come may death to us,
For God has gone away.

War is but a common thing,
Upon our precious lands,
With trees and vimineous plants
And blood spilt on the sand.

And today lifeless souls,
Lie across these plains,
God has left us here to die,
Among the yellow grains.

Matthew Mowat (12)
Torquay Boys' Grammar School

Buy Me A Throne

I woke up on my bench,
A millionaire today.
The stench of success
Extrudes from my pocket.
Last night I had my wrists engraved,
Then bound tight with platinum plastic.
I woke up on my bench today.

I woke up on my sofa,
A few hundred today.
The stench of success
Eroded through my pocket.
Last night I lost my only friend
To bound wrists and platinum plastic.
I woke up on my sofa today.

I woke up in my bed,
Borrowed pennies today.
The stench of success
Excluded from my pocket.
Last night I threw my scars away,
The bound wrists and platinum plastic.
I woke up on my throne today.

Jay Spencer (17)
Torquay Boys' Grammar School

Sculpture Poem

Made out of purest marble,
Four times his normal size.
Soon to be the most amazing sculpture ever made,
Representing his complete imperial power,
Standing higher than all other people looking up at him.

Time passes . . .
His heroic head untouched,
Still powerful, even after his death.
His feet worn down from people worshipping him.
It seems no time has passed.

Time passes . . .
Now a wreck.
His power seems to have all gone.
A new *better* ruler's statue built much higher than the original,
Almost taking the mick.
Still after his body is gone, his eyes are most powerful,
Forgetting the size.

Time passes . . .
The body has recovered.
Architects and historians admire the statue.
The bigger statue now destroyed through war.
The other real statue remains.

Zac Clark (12)
Torquay Boys' Grammar School

The Sea

The sea is a mad, towering monster,
Prowling around the world,
Leaping forwards in great bounds
Before digging its great claws into the sand
And hissing to stop itself.

The irony of this great beast,
Flopping onto the shore with the last of its energy,
Shaking itself.
Cat-like, sleek and beautiful.

Yet it crashes against the rocks,
Scraping its claws down the sheer rock face,
Stone rendered to sand in its paws,
It sprinkles the remains back onto the land
Before rearing up again.

Sailors scream haunting screams,
Taking in their last views of Earth
As they are engulfed by the sea,
The great cat, Cerberus incarnate.
Last thought of loved ones
Before the sea envelops them.

The tiger splashes warm against my feet,
A beautiful turquoise on the white sand.
It tickles playfully. How ironic.

Paul Moroz (11)
Torquay Boys' Grammar School

Hallowe'en

What does he gain
From all the pain?
Why did he kill his sister?
What made him insane?

Is he thick
Or is he sick
And twisted?
He snaps them like tooth picks.

Death is his game
Hell is his name
He is Hell alright
He can't be brought tame.

What does he gain
From all the pain?
Why did he kill his sister?
What made him insane?

He killed all his life
He would likely kill his wife
If he had one
His best weapon is a knife.

His eyes are like Hell
He doesn't have to ring a bell
He walks right in to his other sister
And he doesn't let them tell.

Shaun Minto (13)
Torquay Boys' Grammar School

Equal Opportunity

A ray of hope, values evoked,
Depleted and all on his own,
Anaesthetised, dehumanised,
Outcast, alone from his home.

Gleaming bright eyes, thunderous skies,
Ragged, rough and raw,
Alone on the street, engulfed by the heat,
Alienated and poor.

A fragment of time, contained in the mind,
A friend, the family he knows,
Close to the heart, perceived in the dark,
Longs for emotions to grow.

Leaping away, free from the day,
Image of time obsolete,
Strive for the fight, bright shining light,
Memories of time on the street.

Out from the clouds, sun blazing down,
Vast and lifeless in time,
Back to the day, soon gone, passed away,
Out and now back in the mind.

Where will he go, nobody knows,
Is he determined or free?
Chance to escape, longs for his break,
Visions of a man he could be.

Simon Ward (17)
Torquay Boys' Grammar School

The Emperor's Statue - Set In Stone?

Majestic marble looming high.
Above the heads of men
He holds the Earth, the sea, the sky,
At the centre of this glowing sphere, is Jerusalem
Of diamond bright,
He holds the light,
That shall shine forever,
Amen.

Time passes

The marble, it is chipped and torn,
Without a nose he stands,
He now holds a duller sphere,
With less than perfect hands.

Time passes

An eroded stand,
He falls from grace,
The sphere drops from his hand,
All you can see is the sad residue,
Of the most powerful man in the land.

Time passes

The statue has vanished completely,
All memory of it is erased,
His power is gone, it has crumbled like,
That statue white and glazed.

Mark Buffey (13)
Torquay Boys' Grammar School

Hero Or Not?

No thunder of hooves, stamping along,
Because Blair has banned it so.
No sound of gunshots ringing out,
Blair has said it must go.

So in many eyes he's a hero,
He's stopped the hunters' fun.
But if only he could come to my farm
And see just what he's done.

So my chickens lie there bleeding,
They lie torn limb from limb.
Because Blair has let the foxes out
And it's all down to him.

So Blair well done you're a real hero,
You've stopped the hunter's game.
But did you do so because you cared,
Or did you do it for fame?

So the foxes are free from danger,
But they'll spread like wildfire
And the number of foxes on this land,
Will just get higher and higher.

Oh Tony Blair you're my hero,
You deserve a golden crown.
So thanks to you and your foxes,
My chickens are going down.

Oh Tony Blair your bad ideas,
Are getting more and more.
You've already banned fox hunting
And don't get me started on the war.

David Benson (13)
Torquay Boys' Grammar School

Should The New Dam Be Built?

The old dam does its job quite well,
It's big and sturdy, grey and hard.
It saves the villages small and meek
And stops the flooding, a downstream guard.

But what of villages higher up?
The downstream guard is failing.
They really need another dam,
Or in storms they'll be bailing.

The council meets and makes a plan,
The builders start construction.
But people who enjoy the site,
Think it's scenery mass destruction.

A beautiful place would be flooded,
The cliffs sunk underwater.
'Terrible!' some people cry,
But others say they oughta.

Then SOS Loire Vivante,
Appear upon the scene.
A group to keep the builders out
And keep the Loire dream.

'*Oh no!*' the village people cry,
'Don't wipe the nature out.'
'Don't stop now,' the others say,
'Or *we'll* be flooded out.'

It seems Vivante has won for now,
They keep watch through the night.
It seems people would rather risk,
Their homes and challenge nature's might.

Charlie Hornsby (12)
Torquay Boys' Grammar School

Vampires

Are they myths or are they true?
Is what we do not know
Kids fear them, tell me something new.

Are they our bloodsucking friends?
With sharp, pointed teeth
And long thick nails
Black as a panther
Quick as a cheetah
Silent as a tiger hunting its prey
Strong as a bear
Stalking us every move we make.

Do they kill just for fun?
They live on blood
Biting, sucking, biting
Healing the wound with their spit
Leaving carcasses wherever they tread
Clever like a monkey
Scary like a rhino
Disguised like a chameleon
Hunting us every move we make.

Do they last forever?
Hunters in the moonlight
Hunted in the sunlight
Taking on two personalities
Vampire bats in enclosed spaces
Predators everywhere else.

Check behind your sofa
Check wherever you may go
Be careful, you don't know
You might be . . . *next!*

Matthew West (12)
Torquay Boys' Grammar School

Gunshot In The Wild Wood

Walking their spotted dog
They were in the wild wood
Gunshots could be heard
Just like in the hood.

What could they do?
Little boy dying,
What could he do?
The dad was crying.

Blood gushed onto the path
The little boy fell on the floor
The father saw the blood
This boy may live no more.

What could they do?
Little boy dying,
What could he do?
The dad was crying.

Two men with a gun
You could see a shining light
They saw the boy on the floor
They ran into the night.

What could they do?
Little boy dying,
What could he do?
The dad was crying.

Mistaking the boy for a fox
It was only an accident
It was illegal anyway.
If only they had Clark Kent.

Richard Petty (12)
Torquay Boys' Grammar School

Tony Blair's Heart Scare

Tony Blair had a heart scare,
He went to get it mended,
At Hammersmith Hospital,
Before his life ended.

He had a heart flutter,
So he missed a beat,
He had to have an operation,
To make his heart neat.

He had the treatment,
So he could do his job,
And be Prime Minister,
Not some forgotten slob.

Tony Blair had a heart scare,
He went to get it mended
At Hammersmith Hospital
Before his life ended.

Doctors said a quick recovery,
From the procedure by the NHS,
Although it was free,
It shouldn't be a mess.

Two and a half hours,
Was the operation time,
To use a heart cavity,
To make the heart rhyme.

Tony Blair had a heart scare,
He went to get it mended,
At Hammersmith Hospital,
Before his life ended.

James Bourne (13)
Torquay Boys' Grammar School

Reincarnation

Running in this cycle,
Staring through different eyes,
Being in someone else's shoes,
Seeing the tears, fears and cries.

The obstacles awaiting me,
Blocking the path,
The release of perfection,
Not hatred and wrath.

No clouds can dampen my thoughts,
Inside this invisible spirit dimension,
When I switch my body,
Every memory is an illusion.

Fighting through the very air,
A green light, almost holy,
Shimmering through the canopy of leaves,
The whole world catching my breath.

In the body of a glistening green canopy,
I suck the moisture below,
Yet another life of endurance,
What next I do not know.

I have lived my lives sensibly,
My karma nearing the end,
The long, twisting road ending,
The bright gate of Moksha.

It was a never-ending dream,
Full of wondering of the mean and keen,
I was thinking of everything there could be,
But now I am at perfection.

Thomas Uddin (13)
Torquay Boys' Grammar School

Simple Simon

Pies are meaty, good to chew,
So why did Simon have so few?
Was it because he had no money,
Or did it make his tummy funny?
Why did it leave him feeling sick,
Was it the gravy - far too thick?
Alas! It was none of these,
The culprit if you please,
The pie man that Simon met -
Had baked too few and only let,
Simon have a single pie,
But why did it make Simon die?
Well the pie man was a wicked wizard
And made the pie with chopped up lizard,
Then he evilly cast a spell,
Which hung around and left a smell,
When eaten what this pie would do,
Would make you instantly need to chew!
Not knowing this Simon took the pie
And look what happened, my, oh, my!
His jaws started going *snap, snap, snap!*
Oh *how* Simon wished he could shut his trap,
He tied a belt around his head
And still gnawing, he went off to bed.
Eventually, poor old Simon passed away,
But what happened to the pie man gay?
Well, when he saw Simon, he laughed with glee,
'Ha, ha, ho, ho,' and 'tee, hee, hee!'
I'm warning you this poem is not a lie,
So think before you eat a pie.

Polly Brown (12)
Torquay Grammar School For Girls

Autumn Walk

Flowing river, flowing river,
Push all your problems away.
Flowing river, flowing river,
Alive every day.

Gentle breeze, gentle breeze,
Rustling all the autumn leaves.
Gentle breeze, gentle breeze,
Swaying in the trees.

Floating clouds, floating clouds,
You make the birds sing aloud.
Floating clouds, floating clouds,
Stands out like a single diamond in a crowd.

Rolling mist, rolling mist,
Covering the land.
Rolling mist, rolling mist,
Reaching the seashore and the sand.

Reflected sunlight, reflected sunlight,
Bouncing off the stream.
Reflected sunlight, reflected sunlight,
Butterflies dancing, like in a dream.

Empty fields, empty fields,
The corn has all gone.
Empty fields, empty fields,
The farmer's work is done.

Sunset, sunset,
Another finished day.
Sunset, sunset,
As the sun fades away.

Charlotte Slough (12)
Torquay Grammar School For Girls

Parting

I watch and cry, I see your pain,
Soon you will be asleep
And no one shall ever hurt you,
Yet why do I still weep?

I know that I should try to help
And save your precious life,
Then again to act to save you
Would condemn you to strife.

I cannot bear to stay with you
And suffer years of pain,
Each day repeats the one before,
Where joy I have to feign.

But now the guilt has captured me,
Because I have killed him,
To help or let him slip away,
His light begins to dim.

The house is still, in shadow now,
But why am I upset?
Is it because I've lost the one
I must try to forget?

I will never forgive myself,
For the things I have done,
His pain has passed and is over
While mine has just begun.

Jessica Levinson Young (12)
Torquay Grammar School For Girls

Remember

As I remember a place from my past
I slip from my life to dream
The spice in the air, the blood in the earth
And the tears in the waters of the stream.

I let the water take me now
Under its sparkling waves
I float past the world and all its colours
Begin to wither and fade.

Dappled forest, shattered desert
Show me what I have not seen
I'm weak now and still desire
Something beyond my reach.

I think I will lock my dreams away
One last time
I've lost my will, no reason now
I've forgotten all that is mine.

Remember me . . .

Ellen Harber (12)
Torquay Grammar School For Girls

Wizards And Witches

Wizards and witches,
Ghosts and ghouls,
Casting spells and fighting in duels,
Making potions whilst sitting on stools,
Wizards and witches,
Ghosts and ghouls.

Chloe Avery (12)
Torquay Grammar School For Girls

Shadows Of The Night

Rushing down the corridor of hatred and pains,
Frustration and anger running through your veins,
Rain pouring,
Shadows creeping,
Floods gushing,
Rage leaping,
Wind sweeping,
Thunder blasting,
Life sleeping,
Eyes peeping,
Moon weeping,
Mist seeping,
Total enveloping,
Sight amazing.

Libby Feist (12)
Torquay Grammar School For Girls

Smile

Laughing children having fun, standing in the garden
Outside my house before a birthday party,
The sky as blue as the deep sea,
The garden full of flowers,
The bright green plants, midnight black gate and the bright blue sky.
A summer birthday in June,
Emily carrying a white, plastic bag,
Me poking my tongue out, four friends and my brother,
If I look long enough, I will be able to remember
How much I liked my friends.

Ellie May (11)
Torquay Grammar School For Girls

Christmas Orphan

Wistfully peering through the frosty window,
Shivering in the fallen snow,
She shifted her feet and moved to and fro
Notable to bring herself to go.

Footsteps crunched through the snow, quite nigh,
She held out her pot to this passer-by.
'Come in,' said the voice, 'and don't be shy,
There's a roaring log fire and hot mince pie!'

Once inside it was just as he said,
With four young children snuggled in bed.
She ate some pie and was soon well fed,
Dozing by the fire, happy thoughts in her head.

Deborah Mason (12)
Torquay Grammar School For Girls

Holiday In The Sun

The beginning of a holiday,
A group of cheery children in the black of the night
On the sunny island of Gran Canaria.
My two pretty sisters and me smiling into the camera,
One is cheekily swaying her skirt to the side.
Dark skies above and decorations beaming from behind,
The lights as bright as the sun, shining down on us.
The glossy brown of our hair newly braided.
If I look long enough, I will be able to remember my family all together
Having a great time!

Lauren Perriton (11)
Torquay Grammar School For Girls

The Sky

The sky is red,
The sky is blue.
The birds sing their chorus,
The day is new.

The sky is orange,
The sky is yellow.
The rocks are on fire,
Life is mellow.

The sky is grey,
The sky is mould.
The factories pour out their smoke,
The Earth is old.

The sky is purple,
The sky is black.
The world will soon be destroyed,
Will it ever be back?

Hannah Reeves (12)
Torquay Grammar School For Girls

The Curious Cat

Tail held high like a flagpole,
Ears cocked, sharp to the sky,
Chasing mice to the mouse hole,
Crouching as birds fly by.

Eyes shrewd and clear in the sunlight,
Sniffing with a shiny, wet nose,
Sharp white teeth, sparkling bright,
In the face of a cat who knows.

Elizabeth Hunt (12)
Torquay Grammar School For Girls

Memories Of Summer

As the water lapped and dipped at the soft, smooth sand,
A sailing boat came into the quay.
As the tourists departed the seashore haven,
The sun set over the shining sea.

As the warm day wandered into a cooling night,
The summer came to a pleasant close.
As the migration season of autumn began,
So did the petals fade on the rose.

As summer drifted away, memories are left,
Faint memories of joy and laughter.
As the gentle flowers drooped and shrivelled to brown,
Cold autumn defeated the warm summer.

Charlotte Dyer (12)
Torquay Grammar School For Girls

Lost World Beneath
(Based on Roadford reservoir)

As I sit and wait, flags fly freely around me,
Encircling me, drawing me in.
The water crawls with a new species,
Skimming the water around me.

Whizzing along in the whirling wind,
Tacking, flying, falling in, gybing,
Oblivious to the lost depths below.

For below used to live an enchanted village,
Forgotten, encrusted in gold.
Now lying helplessly at the foot of mercy,
No more than a mythical story to be told.

Sarah Whittaker (12)
Torquay Grammar School For Girls

Season Of Loss

As winter draws more near, more near
And autumn has begun,
The nights get colder, colder still,
The promise of winter fun.

The breeze whistles from leaf to leaf,
As they turn red to gold,
They then fall down and lie, lie still,
Enjoyed by young and old.

As people sit and watch the change,
The change the seasons bring,
One fair maiden cries, she cries,
As robins start to sing.

Her loved one he has
Gone, has gone,
She thinks he will return,
So many times he's gone before,
Her broken heart will burn.

Amy Harding (12)
Torquay Grammar School For Girls

The Invisible Man - Haikus

The man crept slyly,
Lurking in small alleyways,
Hiding in shadows.

Covering his face,
Trying to forget himself
Find a quiet place.

To hide from the world,
No one wants to know this man,
Homeless and alone.

Olivia Mae Jaremi (11)
Torquay Grammar School For Girls

Hallowe'en

H orrified faces at Hallowe'en,
A pple bobbing at my friend's house,
L ights of the fireworks as they bang like pretty patterns in the sky,
L anterns carried by ghostly figures secretly walking down the street,
O range pumpkins shining brightly,
W itches cackling overhead loudly,
E njoy trick or treating round the block,
E ating yummy mouth-watering treacle toffee,
N ightmares of Hallowe'en.

Next year same again:

It's Hallowe'en, it's Hallowe'en,
When little children seem to gleam.

Orange pumpkins shining bright,
It gives some people such a fright.

Light of the fireworks as they bang,
Plastic spiders as they hang.

Witches cackling overhead loudly,
A child wins at the fancy dress party, getting her medal proudly.

Bats flying overhead,
Having nightmares in your bed.

Ellie Wilde (11)
Torquay Grammar School For Girls

The Wedding

A smiling family,
A new husband and wife
All in glamorous dresses and suits
Just standing in the warm sunshine.
A windy April Fool's Day at luxurious Oldway Mansion,
My uncle's hand resting gently on my shoulder,
My beautiful mum and new stepdad and an excited me!
Clear blue skies with flowers swaying in the wind,
Our smiles stretched from ear to ear.
Memories of everyone excited like they were children and
                                              it was Christmas.
Feeling that there was going to be a colourful future.
The golden sun shining on us,
Glossy cream and dazzling blue dresses.
If I look hard enough I will be able to remember
The happiness my mum and I were feeling
About our future with a new family.

Sophia Peutherer (11)
Torquay Grammar School For Girls

Fire

I am fire,
As deadly as a tiger.
I am as dangerous as lightning,
And the sound of screaming destruction.
I feel nothing
When lit
Although alive.
But worst of all . . .
I am your shadow.

Abigail Fryett (12)
Torquay Grammar School For Girls

Love Will Never Die

My love for you is near but yet so far,
It grows every time I look at you,
Your warming love glows like a distant star,
My heart tells me I love you through and through
For every year that we have spent apart
My heart does bleed for loss of time and love
And I do cry every time you depart.
When I see you my heart floats like a dove.
I hope this passion will always sustain,
Your looks and words are carved within my mind.
If you died, then for sure my heart be slain.
With lovers' rope our hearts have been entwined
And from my soul I wish to give to you
Love's sweetest kiss as soft as morning dew.

Amy Goldman (12)
Torquay Grammar School For Girls

Five Girls

Five girls smiling
On a wonderful June day,
Standing outside a campsite on Herm.
Hannah, laughing on the end.
Emilia, trying not to use her broken arm.
Me, feeling sad about leaving.
Katy trying to force her way between Anniliese and Emilia.
The friends, joined together like a chain
And the colours of old, faded clothes worn by children.
If I look long enough, I will be able to remember the reason why
                                                          the photo was taken,
To remember our laughter and the fun we had on those days on Herm.

Serena Gosden (11)
Torquay Grammar School For Girls

Fear In The Forest

Fear swoops through the air
Like a sparrowhawk
Looking out for defenceless prey.
It chooses its moment
And dives down towards the ground.

Fear creeps through the forest
Like a scavenging fox
Silently approaching the chosen victim.
No way out.
It pounces and proclaims the end.

Fear waits in its trap
Like a silent spider
Who spins its web and lingers.
Patiently it awaits the meal
Always still, a deathly presence.

Fear lies in the undergrowth
Like a hissing snake,
Silently slips from side to side.
It sees its target.
Its deadly weapon is about to strike.

Fear floats deceptively
Like an angler's bait,
Seemingly harmless, secretly a killer.
One simple bite
Turns into pitiless self-destruction.

Fear sits in the forest
On the throne of terror,
Rolling over everything that moves,
Controlling all their lives.
Fear is everywhere.

Debbie White (12)
Torquay Grammar School For Girls

Little Girl

The azure ocean flickers like a thousand diamonds in the sun,
She runs through the sun . . . little feet printing the precious sand,
                                      running, fearless,
Innocent blue eyes, seas of imagination,
A world somewhere else.
Little girl in the wind
Around the castles, towers, princesses, knights.
Little girl runs,
Little girl flies.
Sea reflects lines of the past in my face,
Blue eyes, wells of fear and anxiety.
Little girl has gone but I can still see her
Running along the lines in the reflection of my face . . .

Gabriella Strange (16)
Torquay Grammar School For Girls

Memories

During cold March 2004,
In a house in the heart of Dartmoor,
Cheerful children on their way home,
From a fantastic year 6 trip.
While my best friend is trying
To include her beautiful smile,
Harley on her hands and knees
For the camera shouting, 'Cheese!'
Memories, like friends, stay with me for ever
And, if I look long enough,
I will be able to remember
The personalities of my old friends.

Amy Edwards (11)
Torquay Grammar School For Girls

Stolen Love

What punishment is it that I deserve?
For what have I done to sweet, fair life?
For him I have never failed to serve,
For all his wishes I've had to strive,
My lover's heart does not belong to me.
I feel as if my soul is torn apart,
I hate him for from my love he did flee.
My love is punctured with a poisoned dart.
I thought him special when first we did meet,
'Tis his smile and his charm that is deceiving.
When he had my love, on me he did cheat.
A chain of broken hearts he is weaving,
Hated by my body, loved by my soul,
For it was my first true love that he stole.

Sarah Snow (12)
Torquay Grammar School For Girls

I Am

I am your shadow
creeping behind you.
I am like the wind
making swift but
not so noisy steps.
I make the sound of a ghost's cry.
I feel emotional
when I am not with you,
although when I am,
I love to creep behind you and frighten you.
I am a jet-black grudge
that you will never get rid of.

Melissa King (11)
Torquay Grammar School For Girls

Striking Poses

A happy and cheerful girl,
Proud of what she's achieved.
The start of my new future,
On a cold winter's night.
The lively atmosphere of Torquay town,
Just me, looking proud and excited,
Striking poses at the camera,
Hardly noticed at first,
My mum, dancing in the background.
A cosy night, people chattering and cheering,
Noisy, but comforting.
Memories as gentle as a blanket, warm and soft.
Glistening dresses, sparkling in the candlelit room.
Gold, silver, pink and purple.
If I look long enough, I will be able to remember the love
And support from the people around me!

Hannah Williams (11)
Torquay Grammar School For Girls

I Am Anger

I am anger,
As fast as a cheetah,
I am as unforgiving as a tidal wave,
I like the sound of arguments,
I feel bad when I strike
Although I enjoy it.
I am flaring red,
But most of all
I am anger.

Lily Partridge (11)
Torquay Grammar School For Girls

In The Shadows

In the shadows where nobody goes,
In the shadows nobody knows
Of the sinister creature who silently creeps,
Stalks his prey, then halts and leaps.
Nobody knows of this cold-hearted thing,
Creeping about in the shadows.

It makes sure you're alone, then begins to plot,
As you walk into the shadows like a shot.
You do not know what is about to happen,
Then it does and you are forgotten.
Still nobody knows of this cold-hearted thing,
Creeping about in the shadows.

After a while, humanity faints,
And the monster paints evil with the darkest of paints
All over this country, all over this world,
Then the creature moves on and away he is hurled
To end another planet's life
And cause a lot of trouble and strife.
Now everyone knows of this cold-hearted thing,
Creeping about in the shadows.

Vicky Wilton (11)
Torquay Grammar School For Girls

Sunshine Smiles

A smiling group of happy adults, as proud as can be,
A warm summer's day when my future's just begun,
A cosy cottage beside the sea,
The four generations, the ones who made me,
The dress I wear is still treasured upstairs,
The soft, worn out sofa with rips and tears.
Their smiles are like sunshine filling my heart with love
And their kind smiles glisten brightly in the afternoon sun.
If I look long enough, I will be able to remember the way I grew up.

Jessica Woodhead (11)
Torquay Grammar School For Girls

I Am

I am no one,
As blank as the depths of space,
I am nowhere,
I feel nothing,
I have no colour,
But most of all,
I am alone.

What if . . .
I was someone,
As much a person as anyone,
I was somewhere,
I felt something,
But most of all,
I was alive.

What if . . .
I was more than someone,
If I was famous,
If everyone knew I existed,
I was the one everyone wanted to be,
But most of all,
I had friends.

But . . .
I am no one,
As blank as the depths of space,
I am nowhere,
I feel nothing,
I have no colour,
But most of all,
I have dreams.

Kathryn McGhee (11)
Torquay Grammar School For Girls

Early October

A group of young girls grinning smugly,
Early October in the last months of the 90s,
In the Willows, Torquay, a wacky warehouse.
There are Georgia, Lara and Emma,
Then there is Tiffany and, of course, me!
There is one boy with a juice carton, sucking away
                              like it is going to vanish.
The loud atmosphere with hundreds of jolly people,
A hot day in an immense building,
Memories like swords hitting me continuously,
Colourful like a rainbow,
An invasion of mixed colours,
Shining yellow seeping through the sea of bright colours.
If I look long enough, I will be able to see the happiness that
                                          surrounded me.

Kelly Butler (12)
Torquay Grammar School For Girls

First Time Abroad

A happy girl playing joyfully in a sparkling swimming pool,
A warm summer's day in the holidays,
My first time abroad in Ibiza,
I splash around and giggle for the camera,
The clear blue water with light patterns dancing at the bottom
                                          of the pool,
As clear as a blue sky.
The sparkling blue of the pool and white of the tiles glinting
                                          in the sunlight.
You can just see the reflections quivering on the water.
If I look long enough, I will be able to remember my happiness
Of my first time abroad.

Charlotte Davey (11)
Torquay Grammar School For Girls

Beyond The Shadow

Crooked spine bends over,
Lanky legs tangle up,
Hairy arms swinging in time,
Heart pumping - *bump! Bump!*
Eyes twitching side to side,
Mouth not daring to open,
This is the world of life,
Fear sustains the mind!
Hair standing on end,
Nose weighing heavier down,
Ears not picking up any sound,
Toes wriggling for air,
Death strikes - you fall,
Your nails crack open,
The body slows - all is still,
Fear strangles the hope!
Pulse quickens - heart throbbing,
Blood draining out of your mouth,
Eyes click - burn like Hell,
The mind contracts - you're alive!
Arms flow down to the solid hands,
The legs shiver - move away,
You're dragged along - shadows descend,
Life approaches - fear enters -
>You do nothing . . .
>*You run!*

Cicely Wills (11)
Torquay Grammar School For Girls

Memories

Two smiling children on a soft, sandy beach,
With cool, rippling water.
An exotic beach in Dorset.
My loving brother
And me, wrapped in a cosy towel.
Clear blue skies, with not even a wisp of cloud.
Silky sand covering a vast beach.
The ocean shining brightly like a glinting mirror.
Memories
Like silver keys to unlock the past.
Slate blue and khaki brown.
Summer 2003 - the beginning of a great holiday.
If I look long enough,
I will be able to remember
The bubbling happiness and ecstasy
That I felt on that day.
Memories.

Christina Webber (11)
Torquay Grammar School For Girls

Memories Of Friends

A wintry day moving into spring,
The dark green trees upon Dartmoor's hills,
Bright blue skies with wisps of white,
Happy best friends, smiling with glee
Posing for the camera.
Saff in a builder's pose,
With rock climbing belts way too tight,
The memories are as gentle as a trickling river.
If I look long enough, I will be able to remember
The happy times at Pixies Holt.

Anna Burlace (11)
Torquay Grammar School For Girls

Tree

A claw reaching outwards, from its infinitive prison,
Desperately trying to strain out from its home,
Old and seemingly weak with the lack of movement,
Only the cautious feel the awe lingering in the air around
its gnarled fingers,
A chilled hush yet for many goes unnoticed,
Ancient fingers poised, a volcano still for so many years it is ignored,
A sea of fear washes the ground, to be dried by the thought that
Not one of these many millions of beasts, has left its lifelong
waiting form to attack,
A hollow trust that tames the mind, softens the fear
Of something so complex, it in a way is simple,
A tree.

Roxanne Hughes (11)
Torquay Grammar School For Girls

Happy Days

A group of glamorous girls posing in the toilets
At the last daring disco.
One of many memories at my primary school,
With Charlie embarrassed in her short and unfamiliar skirt,
Emily, my best friend, smiley with a cheerful face,
Beth the bin
And me as mad as ever.
Oh, Mellisa holding friends close, not ready to leave them
Even amongst the smelly loos with no decoration
Are memories like a smiley sun
With ghastly grey walls and multicoloured people.
If I look long enough, I will be able to remember the happy days of
primary school.

Sam Urban (11)
Torquay Grammar School For Girls

A Nonsense Poem

This is a poem that makes no sense,
it's pink, it's purple, it's blue,
it's running around in circles
and it's really confusing you.

It's upside down with nonsense
it's totally insane,
it's jumping up and down
again and again.

It's inside out
but feeling fine.
It's back to front
from time to time.

This poem is very exhausting,
I think I'll have a rest,
next time I'll write some sense
yes, that will be the best.

Kristina Homer (11)
Torquay Grammar School For Girls

Primary School Prom

A happy group of girls with amazing party dresses on,
At the end of my primary school, on a warm July evening.
We were outside waiting for our ride,
All my great friends and I posing for the camera.
Lillie's hair blowing gracefully in the wind,
A full car park with no spaces left,
Gorgeous looking girls all glammed up.
Memories like bright colours shining in my face.
Multicoloured dresses everywhere, just like a rainbow.
And if I look long enough, I will be able to remember the happiness
                                    we had that night.

Annabel Seymour (12)
Torquay Grammar School For Girls

The Man

I can hear him now,
He waits at my door,
He wants me, he has come for me.

I can see him now,
He watches at my door,
He wants me, he needs me.

I can sense him now,
He is close to my door,
He wants me, only me, always me.

He can smell my fear,
He knows I can hear him,
He knows I can see him.
He is waiting, he needs me alone.
I hide under the covers,
He cannot see me there, can he?
I am ignoring him.
He will go away,
At least I hope he will.

Hannah Dennison (16)
Torquay Grammar School For Girls

Memories

A group of excited girls, linked before a pulpit,
A last day at primary school before joyful summer days.
A church in a large village tucked away between rolling hills,
Me and my smiling friends all anticipating the days to come.
I'm holding a keyring, a token of the past,
A busy scene, with chatting people grouped together,
Memories as happy as a bounding puppy exploring its new home,
Navy blue and white taking over the scene.
If I look long enough, I will be able to remember my last days with
                                                                  my childhood friends.

Georgina McLennan (11)
Torquay Grammar School For Girls

Fear

The piercing screech of an owl,
The long, low purr of a car,
The tall, dark creak of a tree,
The dim, deceptive shine of the moon,
We all fell silent,
We all moved closer,
Our stroll became a walk which soon
Became a run,
The trees leaned over,
Watched our every move,
Like menacing ogres towering over us,
Finally we came to the safety of the lights,
That surrounded the mansion,
We were safe!
Or so we thought.

Rebecca Stanley (13)
Torquay Grammar School For Girls

Loving Grandad

A tiny little baby, cradled by her grandad,
A baby's very first Christmas.
I'm sitting happily on my loving grandad's lap,
He'd hold me while I was having a lovely baby nap.
We would be sitting on his favourite armchair
In the living room in his house.
The foggy blue sky in the background
Clashes with his warm, tartan blanket.
Memories like faded colours on the black paper of his death.
If I look long enough, I will be able to remember
How much I miss my grandad.

Hollie Dennison (11)
Torquay Grammar School For Girls

Fear

Fear is:
Having no one,
But hearing someone.
Seeing shadows or
Your own possessions turn into
Nightmares.
In the light:
Nothing.
In the dark:
Something,
Anything,
All things dangerous.
No one's there,
Or are they?

Where's the light?
It's not working.
Why is this happening?
Cloth of darkness,
All around.
A whisper in your ear,
What is it saying?
Nothing.
Hot and bothered,
Sweaty sheets.
Something,
Anything.
No one's there,
Or are they?

Haidee Badcott (13)
Torquay Grammar School For Girls

Give Me Your Name

Give me your name and I will never ever forget it,
I shall tell it to the sea,
I will tell everyone and then lock it with a key,
You shall never have to worry, it will always be safe with me.
If only you would give me your name
I wish, I hope, I plead.

Give me your name and your wish will be my command,
I'll tell it to the birds slowly as they land.
I'll shout it over mountains and write it in the sand.
Oh, how I long for your name,
If only you would give it to me,
I shall lock it in my box and throw away the key.

Rebekah Keating (12)
Torquay Grammar School For Girls

Happiness

A smiling child, chirpy and excited,
The final days of my primary childhood,
The smooth, soft sand that sifts between your toes,
Me running to Mum, proud of my new swimming costume,
Anna, my best friend, being cheeky in the background,
And my brother making attempts to run from the waves,
Anna giggling at her brother trying to do handstands.
With the warm breeze blowing on my face,
The sea's froth like white horses charging to shore.
Everything was as blue as the sky, apart from the pale, white skin
   that covered our bodies like a sheet.
If I look hard, I can see the happiness that day brought to me!

Bethany Clarke (11)
Torquay Grammar School For Girls

Fear

The blanket of night,
Wrapped around us,
I clutched it tight,
Would it protect me from fear?

What was that low drone?
I've *got* to run,
As still as stone,
It's slow and silent, fear.

Did you hear that thud?
Silky soft wail,
Cold is my blood,
Louder, louder gets my fear.

I see a dim light,
Through the large trees,
It's still in sight,
It is all over now, fear.

Rosie Gibbes (12)
Torquay Grammar School For Girls

Fear

Haunting, watching
Getting nearer and nearer
Scratching and scraping
Faster and faster
Winds laughing
Shadows mocking
Something there
Scratching and scraping
Getting nearer and nearer
Louder and louder
Quicker and quicker
Then blank.

Victoria Harris (12)
Torquay Grammar School For Girls

I Am

I am a mystery, as sly as the slyest fox
Blacker than the heart of a killer
A cloudy sky
I am as black as black or as
White as white
I sense your fear, your sadness and joy
Which I am not because
I am mystery.

I am a secret
I am whatever colour you want me to be
I am the thing you desire the most
I am also the thing you want to remain unknown
I haunt your thoughts
I poison your mind
I can drive you to insanity
I can be more frightening than the person stalking you
When I want to.

I am a shadow
Following your every move
Whether you like it
Or not
Seeping into empty spaces
Seeping into you
Like an itch you can't get rid of
Forever
For eternity.

Sophie Thompson (12)
Torquay Grammar School For Girls

Mourning A Loss

The white foam horses crash against the sand.
The silver shingle stretches far away.
These charging horses took you from this land.
That fateful memory will always stay.

How can I not think of you, oh your eyes,
Were darkened pools of secrets and denial.
Thinking of your beauty, how my heart cries,
What's hard for you is death for me to smile.

I love your eyes, your smile, your perfect hair,
Oh to see your flawless features, but when?
Of any other girl I'm not aware,
But now you're gone, we'll never meet again.

Forever I'll love you with all my heart,
Till our death do us part, you're gone, we part.

Nathalie Baker (12)
Torquay Grammar School For Girls

A Clear Sky Of Grey

A rainbow coloured crowd,
August, my beginning and my end,
A Cropredy's grey countryside,
My friends, lost among the crowd,
A lady in green watching me,
Clear grey skies, not a cloud in sight,
People like swarms of bees,
Multicoloured outfits, yellow, red and green,
If I look long enough I will be able to remember
                all the happiness I found that day!

Jade Elms (12)
Torquay Grammar School For Girls

Fear

Fingers around your door,
Whispers of the leaves,
Darkness all around,
Moon covered by cloud.
Footsteps behind,
Hedges rustling,
Heart thudding,
    Ground beneath,
        Slipping,
                Sliding,
   Shapes blurring,
Earth laughing,
    Wind blowing,
       Stuck in the middle
            Can't get out!

Helen Bovey (12)
Torquay Grammar School For Girls

Posing Proud

A best friend standing in a dark room,
Time for a last dance which we welcome,
A church hall in which we party hard.
My best friend, Jazzy, is posing proud,
Jazzy's sparkling; she's flying through the night sky,
Dancing on a wooden floor, dark and twinkling,
Memories are soft and sweet,
A cool black against her glossy white top.
If I look long enough, I will be able to remember memories of
Jazzy and me.

Rebecca Polding (12)
Torquay Grammar School For Girls

Fear

Emerging from the unknown,
Dark shadows lurk,
Their menacing shapes expanding in every corner.

Beady eyes stare out of inky blackness,
Watching my heart lurch.
Whispering voices haunt my mind.
How can I escape?

My pulse racing, heart pounding, body tense.
A long gnarled finger taps against the window,
Pushing the heavy cloak of curtain,
Until it swoops across my face.

Like a gargling plug hole,
A thick sea of murky darkness, slowly sucks me into another place;

Another world . . .

Gabriela Lancaster (12)
Torquay Grammar School For Girls

Fear

Fearing failure as I sat my eleven plus,
Butterflies in my stomach caused by anxiety and trepidation,
The exam had just begun.
The feeling of apprehension, nervousness and unease,
The fright and horror that I wouldn't succeed.
A tidal wave of emotions washing over me,
Helpless in the grasp of panic,
Shivers down my spine.
Knowing that when Mum picked me up,
Everything would be fine.
I would have done my best,
And taken my time
The decision would no longer be mine.

Hannah Short (12)
Torquay Grammar School For Girls

Fear

Wild whispers creeping closer,
Between the dark, looming shadows,
Of old yew trees,
Something mysterious,
Something spine-chilling,
Lurking in the darkness,
An ancient power,
Ready to stifle positive thoughts,
Buried in the earth or entwined in trees?
Bigger, breathing, babbling nightmare,
Silence came and claimed the gloom,
Like a light overpowering the blackness,
Ever onward, for evermore,
The wind stopped whistling,
The whispers settled,
Instantly darkness lifted.

Sarah New (12)
Torquay Grammar School For Girls

Natural Colours

A family group enjoying a warm summer's day,
A small Devonshire farm,
Hot and sunny, a day before school life had begun,
An inside farm with many cages,
A rabbit, silently sleeping in the background,
Natural colours, warm and friendly,
Memories as clear as the Mediterranean Sea,
My kind aunty Claire, my gentle grandmother and me,
　　　　　　　　　　　　　　small and innocent.
If I look long enough, I will be able to remember how much
　　　　　　　　　　　　　　　　　　I miss Claire.

Chantelle Lee (11)
Torquay Grammar School For Girls

The War Children

The war children are searching,
Searching for somebody who can help them.
They are making their way through the rubble,
Not knowing where they are going,
Not caring.

The war children are stumbling over injured bodies,
The bodies of people unfortunate enough, to have not reached
                                            a shelter in time

They remember the siren,
The siren that warned them,
The siren that saved their lives.

The war children remember their parents,
One at war, the other . . . lost . . .
They cannot find her,
They need help,
They are getting scared.

The war children are desperate now,
They cannot find anyone.
They wish they had not run away from the shelter,
Maybe their mother was waiting there for them.
Maybe!

The war children are running now,
With their hopes.
They really believe she will be there,
When they get there . . .
Nobody.

Juliet Wheeler (11)
Torquay Grammar School For Girls

The Gathering

Tonight is the night of the gathering,
Under the moonlit sky,
Tonight they meet after millions of years,
They froze as the years went by.

First to arrive is the great Martimus,
Wisest of the oak trees,
He looks like he would be the king of all,
Oh, how right you would be.

Second on the scene is Maple,
As important as she sounds,
She came all the way from Canada country,
Crossing the rivers and downs.

Next to arrive there is Mr Cedar,
He comes from a holy land,
He doesn't believe in doing wrong,
His branch is a helping hand.

Last but not least at all, the Redwood,
As tall as a tree can be,
All the way from America,
He's the tallest, the biggest tree.

So the meeting went on and more trees came,
They talked until morning,
The sun came up and the darkness went away,
They froze while the moon was falling.

Katie Girow (11)
Torquay Grammar School For Girls

My Love

When I am older I shall fall in love,
It will shine brighter than the blazing sun,
A love so clean and pure, just like a dove,
I will laugh a lot and have so much fun.

The glint in his eyes sparkles so brightly,
His words like a melody that's so sweet,
A life without his love, so unsightly,
I simply cannot wait for us to meet.

When it's all over and we love no more,
I shall never love you much, not one bit,
The red rose will not be red anymore,
It is black and in the vase it will sit.

Now I will never fall in love again,
To make sure my heart cannot be broken.

Georgina Picot (12)
Torquay Grammar School For Girls

Memories Like Confetti

A beautifully dressed, smiling pair of children
On a chilly day in February 2004.
My mum's wedding with me as a bridesmaid,
Me looking at the door and my brother in his smart suit,
In a cosy reception room with floral wallpaper,
Memories like confetti floating to the floor,
Satin as red as a rose
And gold in the waistcoats to match.
If I look long enough I will be able to remember . . .
The happiness of having a new beginning!

Victoria Harvey (11)
Torquay Grammar School For Girls

True Love!

Love is like a circle, it never ends,
It makes people happy, but also sad,
It can sometimes start from being good friends,
And untrue lovers can send people mad,
You never forget your first one true love,
But you want to forget the one that lies,
It sends you up to cloud nine and above,
A girl's tears look like diamonds in her eyes,
Without love in your heart there is despair,
If you've found true love there should be no doubt,
My sad broken heart is in disrepair,
Then all you can do is scream and shout,
Without that love you feel like a rag,
No love in your heart makes it start to sag.

Hannah Zebrowski (12)
Torquay Grammar School For Girls

Winter Draws Near

An amazed gang of children admiring the outdoor art,
A tiny slice of autumn crispness
By a peaceful, running stream in Dartington.
Rhia is cold as winter draws near.
I stand crooked, trying to reach out to the heat so near.
Miriam who looks hopefully at a green stick.
Yellow, red and green leaves blow behind me,
A golden leaf in the centre shines like a star.
If I look long enough, I will be able to remember the
Beginning of a new season filled with cheer.

Charlie Bendall (11)
Torquay Grammar School For Girls

My Love For You

My love for you is oh so pure and strong,
You make me happy when my times are grey.
For you I never would do nought that's wrong,
You warm me up like a hot summer's day.
I never feel so sad when you are here,
You always lighten life up like the sun.
You take away and capture all my fear,
Without you life would be deprived of fun.
If there is not any love in your heart,
My wasted heart will still keep loving you.
The time cannot rewind back to the start,
My love will be just as strong, through and through.
I hope your love appears as strong for me,
And so we can live life so happily!

Lottie Smith (12)
Torquay Grammar School For Girls

Happy Child

A smiling, happy child standing in front of a blossom tree,
A lovely summer day,
One that ended my childhood before school.
Outside our house, in our garden, on the grass,
Me as a young child in my very, very pink dress.
I notice that my hands seem to have found their way into my mouth
                                        despite Mum's nagging.
A grassy background with flowers scattered about,
My hair as scruffy as a scarecrow and my dress crumpled.
If I look hard enough,
I will be able to remember the end of my childhood before school.

Harriet Blackborow (11)
Torquay Grammar School For Girls

Shakespearean Sonnet

Your eyes like diamonds, sparkle in the night,
Straight locks, jet-black, sweep down upon your face.
Your soft, sweet skin is a wonderful sight,
The way you move, so smooth, you step with grace.
Although our love only one full moon's length,
It blossoms truly and will never break.
Our love will last with your tremendous strength,
So I will never cheat, your heart at stake.
I'll give my life to love you forever,
Would you surrender all for my deep love?
I'll stay by your side and leave you never,
Our lives fit together like hand to glove.
My friends, they do not love but, you're smart,
They think you are not worthy of my heart.

Natalie Dingle (13)
Torquay Grammar School For Girls

Purr

He had nine lives but he used up three,
First he fell out of a really tall tree,
Second he fell asleep in the washing machine,
It went round and round,
He had a very good clean!
The third he got chased by an oversized dog,
It nearly ate him in one big gulp.

He loves to lap milk and swallow up dinner,
And he loves to curl up in his basket of wicker,
And when it gets to the end of the day,
He sits at the fire purring away!

Jessica Clarke (12)
Torquay Grammar School For Girls

Love Traffic!

As long as I live you'll always be loved,
There is a special place within my heart,
Where you will stay and never be shoved,
We will never be completely apart.
But what you did I never can forget,
You've always belonged to somebody else;
A long time ago, someone you met,
Now you're leaving me for this someone else.
When I was with you I had happiness,
You made me go all funny in the mind;
But now I will have complete loneliness,
Because you don't love me deep down inside.
Love separates into two different lanes,
It causes happiness but also pain!

Victoria Hammond (12)
Torquay Grammar School For Girls

I Am

I am a mysterious creature,
as silent as the night
and as fierce as a charging rhino.

I am a hidden animal,
never to be seen by man,
but angrier than your least favourite teacher.

I am rough and ragged,
cold and dark,
yet as soft as your favourite blanket.

I am a lot of things,
but what am I really?

Jessica Calf (12)
Torquay Grammar School For Girls

I Am

I am Hallowe'en,
As ghostly as a graveyard.
I am as thunderous as a lightning bolt
And the sound of creaky doors.
I feel excited when the dead come out to play and get their revenge.
Although I am Hallowe'en, I get what I want.
I am deadly black,
But most of all,
I can kill.

Vikki Chammings (11)
Torquay Grammar School For Girls

I Am Me

I am me,
As quiet as a mouse,
As small as a daisy
And the sound of the waves.
I am still me
When unseen
But still bright.
Throughout everything
I am still me.

Shannon Gribble (11)
Torquay Grammar School For Girls

Who Am I?

My first's in gear, but not in fear,
My second's in hear, but not in dear,
My third's in moan, but not in mane,
My fourth's in pans, but not in pane,
My fifth's in part, but not in pram,
Now take all the letters and you'll know whooooo I am!

Joanna Beck (11)
Torquay Grammar School For Girls

I Can't Stop Loving You

You are so handsome, nicer than the spring
Summer, winter, autumn are put to shame
You are beautiful like birds on the wing
You even make the sun and snow look lame
Twenty Noels pass but you are still young
For you there is no age, just perfection.
You are as graceful as branches are hung
For you life gives no time for rejection
More colourful than the rainbow you are
With its radiance shining around the world
In the strongest storm you're the golden star
You are the sun that makes the petals unfurl
    Like the world goes around, night into day
    I can't stop loving you in this same way.

Katie Smith (12)
Torquay Grammar School For Girls

Holiday Memories

An excited group of children standing under the fresh, cold waterfall,
A hot summer's day 2003,
The crisp Troodos mountain of Cyprus,
My two cousins and I laughing in the waterfall,
In the foreground a tree root gnarled and knotted,
An icy waterfall surrounded by mountainous rocks,
The grey of the mist with splashing water,
Memories like pink petals blowing in my mind,
If I look long enough, I will be able to remember the true love and
Happiness we had that day.

Faye Dadson (11)
Torquay Grammar School For Girls

He Is . . .

He is the cherry on icing-topped cakes,
He is the light of the roaring red fire,
He is perfection that God sometimes makes,
I can't help but stare and deeply admire,
But alas, his is for one other,
That girl he dreams about every day,
I can't get my heart to love another,
Oh why does he love that Alexa Fay?
What can I do with this leftover love?
There is no filter, it won't be easy,
I need a miracle sent from above,
Anything, but let it be done quickly,
    And all I can do is lie here and cry,
    Writing this sonnet, I give you goodbye.

Jessica Simpson (12)
Torquay Grammar School For Girls

Memories

A relaxed and loving happy family on a
Special fun filled day of a new century.
A snug little house tucked away in the beautiful country.
Mum, my weird brother making faces at me in blue
With Mum's hand linked through my arm, holding me tightly.
Squashed up in a cosy armchair meant for one,
With smiles like big bananas, ripe and juicy.
Memories like bold paint splashed on white paper,
Turquoise blue sparkling like the ocean and
Glossy gold, glinting like the sun.
If I look long enough, I will be able to remember the
Happiness, love and bonding true.

Rebecca Squires (11)
Torquay Grammar School For Girls

I Am Still Waiting

I'm in the phone box, the one in the hall.
Everything is lonely without you.
I've been patiently waiting for your call.
I am lost and I don't know what to do.
Life seems so empty, when you are not here.
I never wanted it to come to this.
I love you so much, it must be clear.
All I can remember is our last kiss.
Time goes so slowly when you're on your own.
Everywhere I go, I can see your face.
So I'm still waiting, just pick up the phone.
I need you to fill up this empty space.
    I walk in the park where we used to meet.
    I just need you back to make me complete.

Matilda Naylor (12)
Torquay Grammar School For Girls

A Memory So Far Away

The beginning of a great marriage,
My nan and grandad sitting together after their wedding,
How good they looked on the hill past the church in the
beautiful sunlight.
No cloud above them, just the blue skies and flowers blooming.
Only a black and white photo remains but also a memory of a great
day that my grandad will never forget.
I think we all remember my nan that way as if we were there smelling
her perfume.
I hadn't been born then but I remember it as if I was there as it is such
a strong memory.
My nan was a beautiful woman married to my grandad.

Michelle Nixon (11)
Torquay Grammar School For Girls

My Last Day

A smartly dressed bunch of cheeky children,
On the last day.
In the dusty hall which has so many memories, for the last time,
Me and my class, looking funny. Stood in rows but joking about.
My friend Laura striking a pose for the camera (as usual!)
The huge wooden hall with sunlight coming through the dirty window.
Memories like dreams gently blowing away.
The sea of green from our uniform,
If I look long enough, I will remember the beautiful memories
Of happiness from my primary school life.

Chloe Holloway (11)
Torquay Grammar School For Girls

I Am

I am your nightmare,
As unwanted as the spider in your bath.
I am out to spoil your sleep,
I'm like a storm ruining your sunny day.
I feel nothing for you,
I am black.
I seep into your mind,
I spark visions in your head.
Worst of all,
You can't get rid of me.

Ellie Hone (11)
Torquay Grammar School For Girls

Fear

A soft whisper spread through the dark woods,
The cold wind whistled through the trees,
Unseen objects stood all around,
What could they be? A great mystery.

Twigs cracked like the snap of a ruler,
Something was moving, something was near,
Leaves rustled like empty crisp packets,
Could anything ever get rid of this fear?

Something was breathing, quietly breathing,
Whispering in a voice, nothing could hide.
It patiently waited until it found,
The perfect moment it felt it could strike.

Vicky Smart (12)
Torquay Grammar School For Girls

Memories!

Laughing, happy children waiting to splash around,
The start of my adventurous holiday,
In sunny Orlando, Florida.
My excited brother,
And giggling me.
Shadowless objects because of the sun's height,
The calm pool with no ripples, waiting to be ruined,
Memories like dancing ballerinas, floating in my mind,
Untouched clear pool blue,
If I look long enough, I will be able to remember the cheery,
Jolly faces of all my family.

Lillie Barnett (11)
Torquay Grammar School For Girls

I'm Looking For My Glasses

I'm looking for my glasses
I'm sure I put them there
I'm looking for my glasses
I'll have to search everywhere

I'm looking for my glasses
Searching from room to room
I'm looking for my glasses
I hope I find them soon

I'm looking for my glasses
I'm back to square one
I'm looking for my glasses
Oh! I've realised what I've done

I'm looking at my glasses
In the mirror above the bed
I'm looking at my glasses
They are on my head!

Hannah Wilce (12)
Trinity School

Home Is Where The Heart Is

Building bricks
Pick up sticks
The mother bird builds her nest
Built with care
Any sticks to spare?
This nest has to be the best.

At home
I'm all alone
Not scared
I'm not a baby
Look at the sign above the door
Home is where the heart is.

Emma Bascombe (12)
Trinity School

There's A Ghost In My House

There's a ghost in my house,
I'm sure that I'm right,
It's quite scary really -
I've heard it at night.

There's a ghost in my house,
I'll find it tomorrow,
My mum's going out,
So its trail I'll follow.

There's a ghost in my house,
Hooray, my mum's left,
There's noises upstairs,
It might just be theft.

There's a ghost in my house,
I'll go and look now,
But I can't, I'm scared,
It could hurt me, ow!

There's a ghost in my house,
I can't move! It's mad,
But maybe, maybe,
The ghost will be sad.

There's a ghost in my house,
Oh brill, my mum's back,
I'll go look tomorrow,
It's great my mum's back!

Alexandra Turner (12)
Trinity School

Unicorn

In the forest of the winged screecher,
Lives a very amazing creature,
Beautiful is every feature,
He is a unicorn.

Running through the fields of mist,
His shining back, the sun has kissed,
His flowing mane is all adrift,
That prancing unicorn.

He is searching for his mare,
That is his one and only care,
He will never find her there,
That distraught unicorn.

The creatures gather all around,
As he fell unto the ground,
For a while there was no sound,
That falling unicorn.

That amazing creature is no more,
He will stay forever on the floor,
He never found what he was looking for,
That poor unicorn.

Rachel Gates (11)
Trinity School

Love

Love is happiness,
Love is a candlelit dinner,
Love is sharing your last Rolo,
Love is being with the one you love,
Love is having hugs and kisses,
Love is understanding,
Love is saying you're sorry.

Katrina Godden (13)
Trinity School

Fruity Fun!

You can't give it a miss,
It's utter bliss.
It's as round as a ball,
But not very tall.
It's got to be an orange!

Hard, tough skin,
When you bite in.
Not very round,
Pile in a mound!
It's a pear!

Fresh and juicy,
It's not at all messy,
Tiny little pips,
It's not for drips!
Apple!

Yellow and sweet,
Stack them up neat,
Long and sticky,
No need to be picky.
It's a banana!

Abby Coombes (12)
Trinity School

The Man

There was a man from France
Who loved to sing and dance
So obsessed with his size
He started to tell lies
And his nose grew as long as a lance.

Kim Rogers (13)
Trinity School

It's Hard To Find Food In Poverty

I awoke in my lowly bed,
And slowly lifted my aching head.
Tiptoeing past my mother old,
Through the door into the cold.

It's hard to live in poverty.

Looking around into the mist,
I raised my round and clenched fist.
To rub the sleep from my eyes,
Then looked up into the cloudy skies.

It's hard to live in poverty.

Walking past the patched-up houses,
Wearing only muddy trousers.
To go into the busy town,
To look high and low and scour around.

It's hard to live in poverty.

Looking inside every bin,
Licking sauce from a spaghetti tin.
Gathering all the scraps I can carry,
My mother shall be as happy as Larry.

It's hard to find food in poverty.

Rebecca Robbins (12)
Trinity School

The Sea Is Like A Cat

The sea is like a cat,
beautiful in every way.
It's as strong as an ox,
but agile and quick.
It purrs and hisses,
like the wind over the moors.

Matthew Childs (13)
Trinity School

The Clock Went Tick

The clock went tick
I ran around like a lunatic
I smashed through doors
Fed the cows on the moors

I went to the beach
Held onto Mum like a leech
Played around in the sand
And cut my hand

The clock went tick
I started feeling sick
I jumped in a taxi
Paid the driver man
I went straight home
And rang my mum on the phone.

Sarah Smith (13)
Trinity School

Poverty In Africa

Flaming fire
Our conditions dire
Poverty and pain
A rich man's gain
Clothes too small
No food at all
Then
Dank darkness
Complete starkness
No warmth, no love
No help from above
And again the sun rises
In Africa.

Jasmin Salmon (12)
Trinity School

Black . . .

The darkness of the night's sky,
The pain and fear in your head,
The thing that you see
When you close your eyes,
The thing that you see
When you're dead.
The way that you feel
When you're feeling down
Like when somebody else
Is wearing your crown.
The way that you hate
The lies that aren't true,
The way people tell them
And they're all about you.
It's the colour that makes you
Feel so scared,
Like the colour of the murderer
That never cared.

Ashley Ladd (13)
Trinity School

The Tramp

There he lies solemnly,
Rats eating at his socks,
His back propped up properly,
His old watch tick-tocks.
His dog smiles big,
His box is from the shop,
He nibbles on his fig,
He drinks fizzy pop.
He runs like a girl,
His hair likes to curl,
His name is unknown!

Charlie Penny (13)
Trinity School

Wolves

Wolves ran through the hills,
As they ran the crows flew,
They are getting closer,
Nearer and nearer,
Closer every minute.

Their prey was still,
Still as a leaf,
Not a clue,
The wolves were near,
Very near.

Then the prey saw,
And ran,
The chase began,
It dodged in and out
Of the trees.

The wolves gained on it,
The prey could not run further,
Then at a snap of a twig,
It was dead.

The wolves ran through the hill.

Jess Whitworth (14)
Trinity School

Frankie

My fish is orange,
he floats around all light and airy,
just like a fairy.

My fish bubbles all day long,
like he is trying to sing a fishy song.
All he does is eat his calcium flakes,
he wouldn't get his flakes if he lived in a lake,
but his water is clean and clear.

James Hatch (13)
Trinity School

My Cat

I have a cat named Patches
She loves to give me scratches
She runs like a bull
And eats till she is full
She loves to play
With her toys all day
She attacks my feet
And jumps on the computer keys
She jumps at the door
So she sees all
She gets mad when it's time for bed
Until she gets tired and wants to be fed
When she sleeps we all get a rest.

Graham Gilmour (14)
Trinity School

I Think I'm Growing A Tail

I think I'm growing a tail,
I can feel a small lump on my bum,
What have I done to be cursed with a tail,
Why can't anyone tell me what I have done.

I told my brother about my tail,
Then he fell on the ground and laughed,
Then he got back up in front of me,
And told me how I was stupid and daft.

He told me that I don't have a tail,
But there is a small lump on my rear,
It's from a time when we did have a tail,
Thank goodness it's no longer here.

William Doble (13)
Trinity School

The Way I Was Before

I wanted to be noticed,
Standing out in the crowd,
People used to look at me,
And say I was oh . . . so loud.
I don't really care what people think,
And I'm not ashamed that I like the colour pink.
I just wanted to be noticed (not by the way I looked),
I just wanted to scream and shout - but that still wasn't enough.
But now I'm shy and quiet,
People talk to me more
'I just so didn't like the way I was *before*'.

Gemma Edgecombe (13)
Trinity School

Love

Love is a sensational feeling,
Love can be for life,
Love is all around,
Love can hurt or heal.

Love can make you feel whole,
Love comes from the heart,
Love can change your life,
Love is a many wonderful thing.

Emma Long (13)
Trinity School

Under The Sea

Under the sea is better than on the shore
Out in the sun they work all day
Under the sea they slave away
The monsters aren't happy
Guess who's going the other way
Under the sea, under the sea.

Lewys Tapscott Nott (13)
Woodlands School

The New Teacher

It's the first day back at school,
I have got a new teacher,
She has started a new job here,
We are scared of her.

It's the first day back at school,
I have got a new teacher,
She is the witch of the school,
And she doesn't know her maths.

It's the first day back at school,
I have got a new teacher,
She has got a big nose,
And warts on her face.

It's the first day back at school,
I have got a new teacher,
She gives us the cane,
If we don't do our work.

It's the first day back at school,
I have got a new teacher,
She has no name and she's Austrian,
She teaches cookery and cooks rabbit cake.

Ashley Card (13)
Woodlands School

Keith

K is for kind
E is for enthusiastic
I is for interrupting
T is for tiger
H is for hulk.

Keith Persey (13)
Woodlands School

Quad Bikes

On the quad, down the hill,
Over the bumps,
What a thrill!
         Vrrrm! Vrrrm! Vrrrm!

Went to the quad bike place,
Drove around the track.
Had lots of fun,
Like to go back.
         Rrrrm! Rrrrm! Rrrrm!

In a big car park,
Down by the car wash place,
Right by McDonald's,
That's where we race.
         Brrrm! Brrrm! Brrrm!

Ben Morfey (11)
Woodlands School

Let's Count

Give it 1 - let's eat the bun
Give it 2 - I'm feeling blue
Give it 3 - the garden pea
Give it 4 - drink through the straw
Give it 5 - I'm going to dive
Give it 6 - throw the sticks
Give it 7 - up in Heaven
Give it 8 - don't be late
Give it 9 - hang the washing on the line
Give it 10 - let's use the pen.

Claire Jury (12)
Woodlands School

Planes

I'm flying it,
I'm taking off,
It's *noisy!*
I don't know what buttons to press,
I'm on my own,
Help!

I pull a lever,
It goes up,
It's *loud!*
I press a red button,
The wheels go in,
Brilliant!

Flying over the top of clouds,
It's going fast,
It's very quiet,
It's the Concorde,
We land in New York Airport -
Happy!

Reece Dorrall (12)
Woodlands School

The Car

Nana drives Jemma
In her bright red car.
To the shops we go,
Brum, brum, brum.

Driving to see Mum,
It's a long way to go.
Along the road we travel far,
Passing caravans in our car.
Brum, brum, brum.

Jemma Watts (11)
Woodlands School

Lots To Do

Give it 1 - let's have fun.
Give it 2 - lots to do.
Give it 3 - climb the tree.
Give it 4 - roll on the floor.
Give it 5 - we're alive!
Give it 6 - throw some sticks.
Give it 7 - down in Devon.
Give it 8 - coming out mate?
Give it 9 - feeling fine.
Give it 10 - 'Bedtime,' Ben.

Josh Morfey (11)
Woodlands School

In The Car

In the car we go,
Mummy drives s-l-o-w.
To netball we go,
Under the bridge so low.

In the car we go,
To watch Steve play football.
Over hills we go,
Passing cars red and blue.

Kieran Double (11)
Woodlands School